IMAGES OF WAR

ROMMEL'S GHOST DIVISION: VICTORY IN THE WEST

RARE PHOTOGRAPHS FROM WARTIME ARCHIVES

IMAGES OF WAR

ROMMEL'S GHOST DIVISION: VICTORY IN THE WEST

RARE PHOTOGRAPHS FROM WARTIME ARCHIVES

DAVID MITCHELHILL-GREEN

Pen & Sword
MILITARY

First published in Great Britain in 2024 by
PEN & SWORD MILITARY
An imprint of
Pen & Sword Books Ltd
Yorkshire – Philadelphia

ISBN 978 1 39907 805 4

A CIP catalogue record for this book is available from the British Library.

Printed and bound in the UK by CPI Group (UK) Ltd, Croydon, CR0 4YY

MIX
Paper | Supporting responsible forestry
FSC® C013604

Pen & Sword Books Limited incorporates the imprints of Atlas, Archaeology, Aviation, Discovery, Family History, Fiction, History, Maritime, Military, Military Classics, Politics, Select, Transport, True Crime, Air World, Frontline Publishing, Leo Cooper, Remember When, Seaforth Publishing, The Praetorian Press, Wharncliffe Local History, Wharncliffe Transport, Wharncliffe True Crime and White Owl.

For a complete list of Pen & Sword titles please contact

PEN & SWORD BOOKS LIMITED
47 Church Street, Barnsley, South Yorkshire, S70 2AS, England
E-mail: enquiries@pen-and-sword.co.uk
Website: www.pen-and-sword.co.uk
Or
PEN AND SWORD BOOKS
1950 Lawrence Road, Havertown, PA 19083, USA
E-mail: uspen-and-sword@casematepublishers.com
Website: www.penandswordbooks.com

Contents

Acknowledgements

My sincere appreciation is extended to the following individuals who generously shared their knowledge to make this book possible: Sébastien Haule, Dr Thierry Moné, Bertram Nold, and Hiliary Louis Doyle. I am also indebted to Linne Matthews for her expert editorial eye. Many thanks to the enthusiastic staff of Pen & Sword, Roni Wilkinson, Matt Jones and Jon Wilkinson, for championing history and making this book possible.

Notes on Photography and Sources

The German Army collated detailed daily records into *Kriegstagebücher* (or KTBs). Rommel also kept his own personal diary, delegating his aides to update it. He also instructed his staff to keep copies of all his orders, reports and maps. This material, he explained to his friend Kurt Hesse, would feature in a sequel to his earlier *Infanterie greift an* (*Infantry Attacks*), a First World War memoir. Rommel was a keen photographer, and by the end of the campaign had taken and amassed hundreds of photographs. Most of the images used in this book are drawn from the 'Rommel Collection', seized after the war and today held in the US National Archives and Records Administration (NARA).

Rommel pictured holding his Leica camera, a gift from Reichspropagandaminister Joseph Goebbels. An ardent photographer, he often requested that his ADC take images that included him.

Abbreviations, Conventions and Definitions

ADC	aide-de-camp
Ausführung/Ausf	model/type
BEF	British Expeditionary Force
Befehlswagen	command tank
Flak	*Flugzeugabwehrkanone* or anti-aircraft gun
HE	high explosive
Kriegsberichterstatter	war correspondent
Leichter Funkpanzerwagen	light radio armoured vehicle
Leichter Panzerspähwagen	light reconnaissance armoured car
Luftwaffe	the German Air Force
OKH	Oberkommando des Heeres (German Army High Command)
OKW	Oberkommando der Wehrmacht (the Supreme Armed Forces Command)
Pak	*Panzerabwehrkanone* or anti-tank gun
Panzerkampfwagen	'armoured fighting vehicle', abbreviated as Pz.Kpfw. or Panzer
Panzerjäger Abteilung	'tank-hunting battalion'
RAF	Royal Air Force
Reichswehr	German armed forces in the Weimar Republc.
RN	Royal Navy
Reichspropagandaminister	Minister of propaganda
Sonderkraftfahrzeug	'special-purpose vehicle', an ordnance number, abbreviated as Sd.Kfz.
Stuka	*Sturzkampfflugzeug* ('dive-bomber')
Verbandskennzeichen	operational code
Wehrmacht	German Armed Forces

Introduction

Newly decorated, Leutnant Erwin Rommel wears the *Pour le Mérite*, Imperial Germany's highest gallantry award, and *Eisernes Kreuz 1. Klasse* (Iron Cross, First Class).

This book is the story of General Erwin Rommel's 7th Panzer Division – dubbed the 'Ghost Division' – as told through his personal photographic collection, during the latter part of the 1940 Battle of France.

Born at Heidenheim, in the southern German state of Baden-Württemberg, on 15 November 1891, Erwin Johannes Eugen Rommel was the son of a schoolteacher. Breaking from family tradition, he joined the army, entering the 124th Württemberg Infantry Regiment as an officer cadet in 1910, aged 18. Commissioned as a Leutnant on 27 January 1912, Rommel fought in France, Romania and Italy during the First World War, displaying an aptitude for leadership. Serving with distinction in the Alpenkorps (Alpine Corps) at the Battle of Caporetto (October to November 1917) and in the capture of Longarone on 9 November, he was awarded the coveted *Pour le Mérite*.

One of 4,000 officers retained in the Weimar Republic's Reichswehr after the November 1918 Armistice, Rommel was initially assigned to the 13th Infantry Regiment in October 1929. A subsequent posting as tactics commander in the *Infanterieschule* (Infantry School) marked a turning point in his career, leading to several instructor roles. A textbook based on his tactical lecture notes, *Gefechts-Aufgaben für Zug und Kompanie* (*Combat Problems for Platoon and Company*), published in 1934, was followed by *Infanterie greift an* (*Infantry Attacks*) in 1937. The second volume, which drew heavily

Rommel's 1937 book *Infanterie greift an* (*Infantry Attacks*) combined his First World War experience in battle with ideas on military training. By 1945, it had sold 500,000 copies.

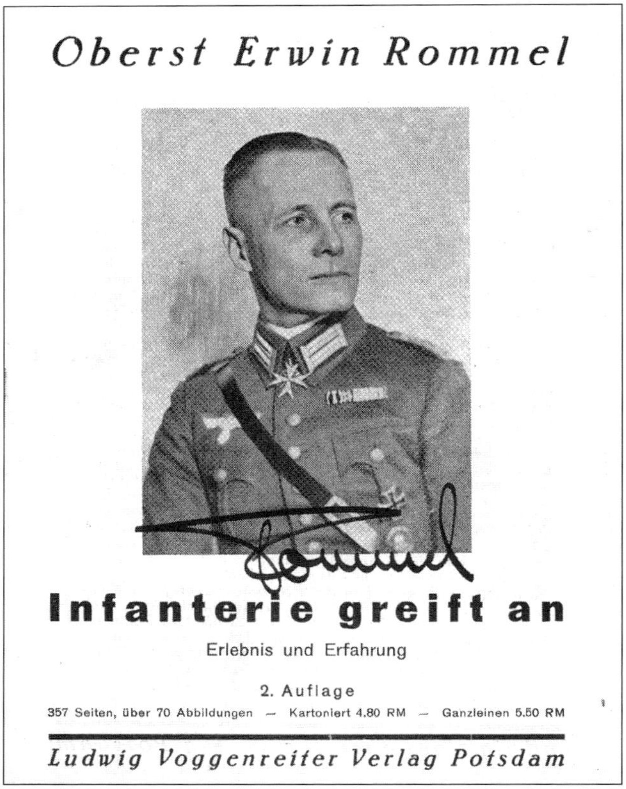

Oberst Erwin Rommel

Infanterie greift an

Erlebnis und Erfahrung

2. Auflage

357 Seiten, über 70 Abbildungen — Kartoniert 4.80 RM — Ganzleinen 5.50 RM

Ludwig Voggenreiter Verlag Potsdam

As Kommandant des Führerhauptquartiers, Rommel led Hitler's personal escort during the Polish campaign. Note the cuff title on his left sleeve.

Rommel in summer uniform with his wife, Lucia Maria 'Lucie' or 'Lu' (née Mollin). The couple met in 1911, while Rommel was in Danzig attending the officer cadet school.

Rommel, seen here on leave, skirted protocol through a direct appeal to Hitler for command of a Panzer division, though admitting 'many others were more qualified'.

on Rommel's lecture notes and experiences during the First World War, caught Adolf Hitler's attention, as did a commendation from Nicolaus von Below, a former student now serving as Hitler's Luftwaffe adjutant. A series of roles and promotions followed. Assigned as liaison officer in charge of Hitler Youth military training to the War Ministry, he was reassigned as commandant of the Theresian Military Academy in Austria. Promoted to Generalmajor in August 1939, Rommel commanded Hitler's personal security battalion, the Führerbegleitbataillon, and his personal escort during the 1939 invasion of Poland.

At the conclusion of the Polish campaign, Rommel successfully approached the Führer to lead a Panzer division, a decision raising eyebrows in Berlin. Alfred Jodl, chief of Hitler's armed forces high command (Oberkommando der Wehrmacht, or OKW), was 'flabbergasted at my new posting', Rommel confided to his wife, Lu. Arriving at Bad Godesberg, on the Rhine, on 10 February 1940, an ambitious Rommel assumed command of the 7th Panzer Division.

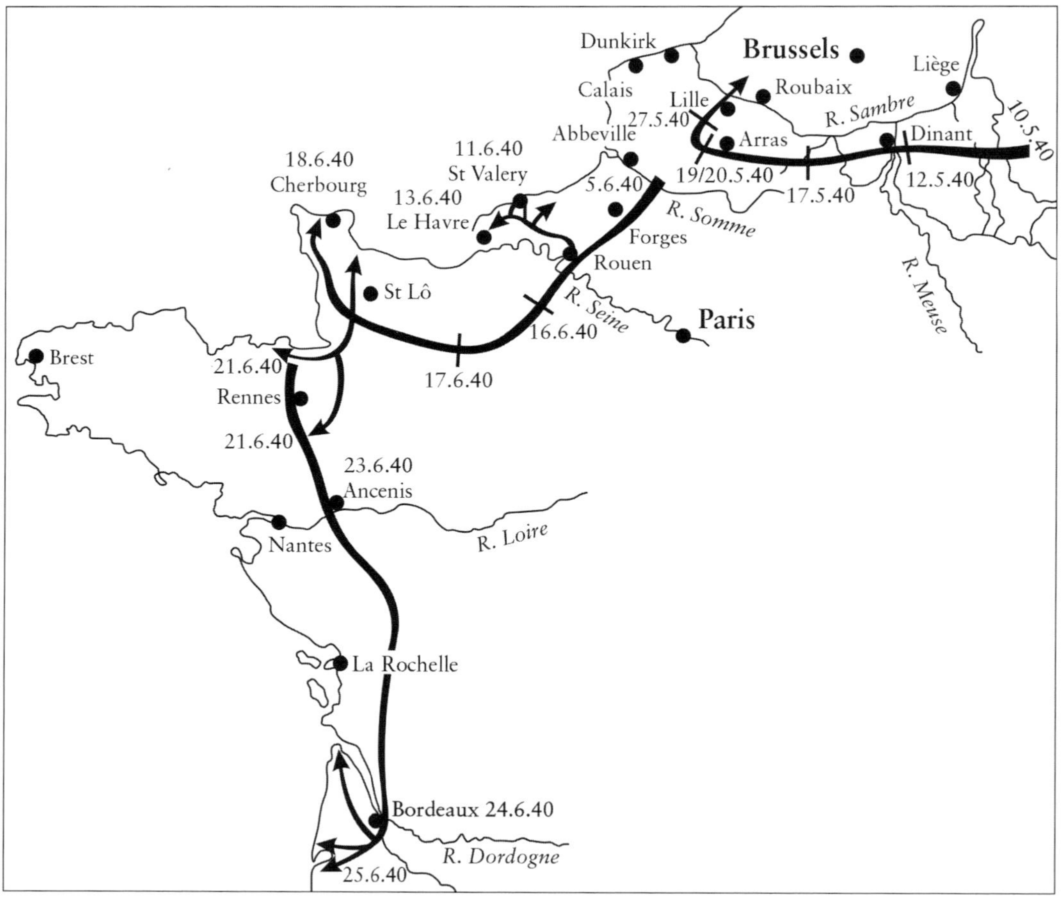

The route taken by the 7th Panzer Division, 10 May to 25 June 1940.

Part I

Chapter One

Hitler Strikes West

Twenty-one years after silence fell across the Western Front, Europe was again gripped by war. Hostilities erupted on 1 September 1939 following Adolf Hitler's invasion of Poland. France and Britain, as Warsaw's allies, declared war on Germany two days later. The French launched a minor offensive into Western Germany on 4 September, losing 2,000 men, before Général d'armée Maurice Gamelin ordered all troops to retire to their positions behind the Maginot Line.

A period of non-belligerent inactivity in the west followed, labelled variously as the 'Phoney War', 'bore war' or '*Sitzkrieg*'. The Allies' rejection of Germany's loose peace entreaty of 6 October 1939 persuaded Hitler to eliminate France as a threat and remove Britain's Expeditionary Force (BEF) from the Continent. The French military, on paper at least, presented a powerful force, fielding more tanks and artillery than the Germans. France's famous Maginot Line also shielded key industrial areas and favoured a German attack through Belgium. Haunted by the horrendous loss of life in the First World War, many French politicians and military leaders, including Général d'armée Maurice Gamelin, sought a confrontation beyond their border that could somehow spare more bloodshed. Hostilities recommenced on 9 April 1940 with Hitler's invasion of Denmark and Norway, undertaken to secure iron ore shipments from Sweden and to pre-empt an Allied invasion. A month later, 10 May 1940, the Führer launched *Fall Gelb* ('Case Yellow') – an offensive against neutral Luxembourg, Holland, Belgium and France.

Initially deceived into believing the main weight of the German thrust was targeting southern Holland and northern Belgium, French forces and the BEF moved northwards into Belgium. In a daring move that caught the defending French by surprise, Generaloberst Gerd Rundstedt's Army Group A pushed through the rugged and densely wooded Ardennes region into south-east Belgium. Spearheading Generalleutnant Hermann Hoth's XV Corps, Generalmajor Rommel's 7th Panzer Division (see Appendix 1) reached the Meuse River, a formidable barrier, opposite the village of Dinant, on the afternoon of 12 May. Encountering considerable resistance, Rommel was at the forefront of the river crossing and subsequent breakout towards the French frontier. With the 7th Panzer Division rupturing General André Corap's IXe Armée (9th Army), General Heinz Guderian's 2nd Panzer Division captured two vital bridges across the Ardennes Canal while General Georg-Hans Reinhardt's XXXXI Panzer Corps crossed the Meuse

French troops in Lauterbach during the French Army's limited incursion into south-west Germany – 7 September to 17 October 1939. History may have run a different course had the French attacked in force, as former Chief of the General Staff, Siegfried Westphal proposed after the war. 'With their very strong superiority … the German forces in the so-called Western Front could stand no more than one or two weeks.' At this time there 'was not a single [German] tank' available there.

and began advancing west towards the coast. Distraught, French Prime Minister Paul Reynaud telephoned Winston Churchill on 15 May, advising his British counterpart of the German breakthrough in the Sedan: 'We have been defeated. We are beaten; we have lost.' Reynaud's cause was not helped by news of the Dutch surrender on 18 May; Belgium capitulated ten days later.

The German offensive may have been held up had the French heeded intelligence warnings of a German drive through the forested Ardennes regions and not rushed their best formations into Belgium. Slowing the German onslaught may have avoided the ensuing encirclement while better tactical control could have delivered more efficient counterattacks.

A 10.5cm le FH18 howitzer from the 78th Artillery Regiment on the eastern bank of the Meuse River shells French positions in preparation for the crossing.

Driving across the border near Clairfayts on the evening of 16 May, Rommel took the initiative and surged through the Maginot Line's northern extension – a chain of pillboxes, anti-tank obstacles and belts of barbed wire. 'We were through the Maginot Line!' he later narrated. 'It was hardly conceivable.' The highly decorated infantry leader, in his first role as a divisional tank commander, quickly proved his mettle, directing his armour in a manner reminiscent of the infiltration tactics he employed during the Great War. A master of manoeuvre, Rommel's unorthodox handling of the 7th Panzer Division

Anti-tank-ditches and barbed wire barriers, resembling a First World War trench line, linked blockhouses along the Maginot Line extension.

Hotchkiss H39 tanks on avenue du 84e Régiment d'Infanterie, Avesnes-sur-Helpe, knocked out during the bitter fighting on the night of 16–17 May 1940.

German infantry watch as Rommel's light armour passes through Le Cateau, heading north-west towards Cambrai and Arras. Leutnant Alfred Tschimpke applauded the role of tanks in his 1940 Nazi propaganda book, *Die Gespenster-Division. Mit der Panzerwaffe durch Belgien und Frankreich (The Ghost Division. With the Panzerwaffe through Belgium into France)*, noting how surprise was one key to success. 'The other lies in their penetrating power. They have no respect for traditional tactical concepts. Where they are set, they break through. Reverse – they don't know that word. It has been so in every period of this war, and so it will be in the future.'

frequently confused his more methodical French adversaries, creating havoc and allowing his tanks to relentlessly press ahead.

Beginning an audacious armoured dash in northern France, Rommel pushed through Avesnes-sur-Helpe, securing the bridge over the Sambre River in Landrecies. 'Civilians and French troops,' he later wrote, 'their faces distorted in terror, lay huddled in ditches, alongside hedges and in every hollow beside the road. We passed refugee columns, the carts abandoned by their owners, who fled in panic into the fields.' It would become a familiar sight. For a period, Rommel outpaced a party of accompanying war correspondents. 'He was always ten miles ahead of us,' friend and former lecturer Oberst Kurt Hesse recalled.

> Once French forces, including tanks, had already pushed in between the little advance party with which he spearheaded his attack and the main force of his division. Even this did not stop him from just driving ahead. 'They will just have to battle through as best they can,' was his only comment.

Hesse was shocked at the scenes following Rommel's advance.

> His tanks had run into a French division coming down the same road, and they just kept advancing right on past it. For the next five or six miles there were hundreds of trucks and tanks, some driven into ditches, others burned out, many still carrying dead and injured. More and more Frenchmen came out of the fields and woods with abject fear on their faces and their hands in the air. From up front came the short, sharp crack of the guns of our tanks, which Rommel was personally directing – standing upright in his armoured command vehicle with two staff officers, his cap pushed back, urging everyone ahead. A *feu sacre* [holy fire] inflamed him: he brooked no opposition from friend or foe. If somebody could not keep up, then let him stand back if only he, Rommel, and two or three tanks could reach the river Somme.

At enormous risk, with elements of his division stretching back to beyond the Maginot Line, Rommel moved through Cambrai to a position south of Arras. At the same time, General Heinz Guderian's tanks reached Abbeville, some 20 miles (30km) from the coast. Confronted by the offensive's unexpected success, Hitler grew increasingly nervous. 'He is afraid to take any chances and so he would rather pull the reins on us,' General Franz Halder, chief of the Oberkommando des Heeres staff (German Army High Command), diarised on 17 May. 'Puts forward the excuse that it is all because of his concern for the left flank!' Halder later wrote of the Führer raging and screaming about imminent defeat the next day. Rommel, meanwhile, continued his derring-do thrust, having already advanced 175 miles (280km) from the Belgian frontier. However, a potentially catastrophic situation had developed. Few motorised infantry divisions were available to secure the expanding territory overrun by the tanks. The closer the Panzer columns were to the English Channel, the greater the distance became for the trailing infantry divisions, sometimes marching on foot, and now several days behind. The German 'corridor' near Arras, Winston Churchill identified, was an ideal spot for the Allies to strike.

A crisis erupted within the German High Command after British armour attacked the 7th Panzer Division outside Arras on 21 May. Rommel was quick to intervene, directing anti-tank guns and 8.8cm Flak guns that helped stem the enemy advance. His exaggerated report of 'hundreds of enemy tanks', however, may well have contributed to Generaloberst Gerd Rundstedt's cautious directive, issued with Hitler's approval, for Allied troops around Arras to be overcome before the advance to the coast could continue. 'For a short time,' von Rundstedt later reflected, 'it was feared that our armoured divisions would be cut off before the infantry divisions could come up to support them.' Perhaps Hitler sought to safeguard his precious Panzer divisions for future undertakings, having lost 753 tanks during the May–June period alone. Whatever the rationale, Hitler's infamous 'halt' order of 24 May, in tandem with a depleted Luftwaffe operating from distant airfields and extended supply lines, helped spare retreating British columns from a certain *coup de grâce*.

Whitehall ordered the evacuation of British forces from the beaches of Dunkirk on 26 May. Hitler repealed his 'Halt Order' the same afternoon, allowing German troops to resume their offensive. The Führer also directed Oberleutnant Karl Hanke to award

Leutnant Paul Lauterbach's Pz.Kpfw. 38(t) was knocked out during the fighting at Haute-Avesnes on 21 May 1940. Note the black Panzer beret on the wooden cross marking Lauterbach's grave. Although the 7th Panzer Division contained a single tank regiment, in place of the normal two, it had three battalions instead of two – a total of 218 tanks, just over half of which were Czech-built Pz.Kpfw. 38(t)s.

Rommel the *Ritterkreuz* (Knight's Cross of the Iron Cross) – his reputation as a Panzer commander firmly established. To the French, the 7th Panzer Division had become the 'Ghost Division' for appearing suddenly and unexpectedly; in German parlance, it was Die Gespenster-Division. To date, Rommel had lost 27 officers killed or wounded plus 1,500 non-commissioned officers and troops killed or wounded – roughly 12 per cent casualties – and a figure Rommel deemed 'very little compared with what's been achieved'. In an interim dispatch, he recorded how his division had captured 6,849 prisoners, taken 48 light tanks, and destroyed 295 light and 18 heavy tanks. 'Not bad for Thuringians,' he exclaimed to his wife (Thuringians were not usually recognised for their military prowess).

The 7th Panzer Division's 7th Rifle Regiment arrived at La Bassée canal on the evening of 26 May. Arriving early the next morning, Rommel found the bridges between Béthune and La Bassée destroyed. Sunken barges cluttered the waterway with accurate sniper fire emanating from the opposite bank. While pontoon bridges were constructed, 'Rommel stood like a target on the embankment and directed fire, while next to him men were being wounded and even killed.' Yet again, Hauptmann Hans von Luck recounted, 'He spurred us on with his exemplary behaviour.' After crossing the canal, Rommel's 25th Panzer Regiment encountered considerable resistance from Allied troops holding a line from Lille to Saint-Omer. Organising a defence line against the Lille garrison, the British troops Rommel earlier encountered at La Bassée had withdrawn northwards while a perimeter was established around Dunkirk. Bravely plying the Channel under Luftwaffe and coastal battery assault, a motley armada of 848 civilian and military vessels in Operation Dynamo successfully brought some 338,226 troops to Britain. The remaining French divisions were brought back across the Somme for a final stand.

A Pz.Kpfw. II completes the canal crossing at La Bassée on a newly constructed pontoon bridge. Note the sunken barge in the foreground.

German armoured cars negotiate the Cuinchy locks at the Canal d'Aire à la Bassée. British snipers had used the lockhouse in the background during the fighting. 'I was able to see for myself how effective our fire had been when we moved back again across the canal two days later,' Rommel recounted.

Wounded BEF troops evacuated from Dunkirk disembark at Dover on 31 May 1940.

Chapter Two

Victory at Saint-Valery-en-Caux

On 31 May, OKW issued a directive codenamed *Fall Rot* (Case Red) outlining the next phase of the German offensive: a two-pronged approach involving an attack by Generaloberst Fedor von Bock's Army Group B (which now included Hoth's XV Corps with the 5th and 7th Panzer Divisions) that would drive across the Somme while a new offensive by Army Group A South would cross the Aisne River towards Paris. Regrouping after the evacuation of the BEF and more than a million Allied troops taken prisoner, a last-ditch French defensive front, the Weygand Line, was established along the Somme and Aisne rivers.

'Storm over the Somme'

'A new chapter lies ahead of us,' Leutnant Alfred Tschimpke chronicled in his 1940 Nazi propaganda book *Die Gespenster-Division*.

> This time the name is Somme. Somme meant blood, iron, destruction for all First World War soldiers. Anyone who had been at Verdun or had fought in the Battles of the Somme knew the war in its most devastating form. … The dirty, blackish river that runs through the green terrain below the high bank slopes, that is the Somme. It looks so harmless, no more threatening than other rivers. And yet, back then, a quarter of a century ago, tens of thousands and tens of thousands walked the path through hell.

Resuming the offensive after six days' rest and re-equipping, the 7th Panzer Division attacked along the Somme at dawn on 5 June. 'We've had plenty of time and so everything, so far as can be foreseen, is well prepared,' Rommel informed his wife, confidently adding that he hoped the war would end in a fortnight. An 'extraordinarily impressive' preparatory barrage preceded the attack, the later discovery of dead and wounded Frenchmen confirming its effectiveness. Providence again smiled on Rommel with a pair of rail and road canal bridges seized that French defenders had failed to destroy (in the hope of regaining the offensive). With rails and sleepers removed, his division's armour and soft-skinned vehicles quickly bypassed the river and surrounding marshy belt. The

Still from a wartime German documentary depicting the French Weygand Line. General Maxime Weygand's order of 26 May urged his men to show aggression against the invading army: 'If the enemy succeeds in making one of those bridgeheads in our front which he uses to push tanks there and then move on to the armoured attack, it is necessary, however small this bridgehead, to immediately reject the enemy on its lines by crushing it under the fires of artillery and aviation and by counterattacking.'

subsequent fighting was heaviest near the village of Hangest-sur-Somme, stubbornly defended by a battalion of French colonial troops.

Unlike the opening days of *Fall Gelb*, the 7th Panzer Division pushed ahead across wide open fields in a *Flächenmarsch* or 'formation drive' manoeuvre – armour leading and protecting the rifle regiments, anti-tank and reconnaissance battalions bringing up the rear.

By 7 June, it had travelled over 40 miles (64km) beyond the Somme, splitting the French Tenth Army. A French woman at Elbuef rushed to the German general, asking, '*Vous êtes anglais?*' ('Are you English?'). Shaking his head, she screamed and disappeared back inside her house. Two days later, on 9 June, Rommel reached the Seine, though blown bridges checked his advance for the moment. With General Hoth ordered to intercept Franco-British forces retreating towards Le Havre, the 7th Panzer Division was directed to seize the port. Rommel, in the meantime, reached the coast on 10 June. 'With my signals section I drove on in advance of the regiment through Les Petites-Dalles and down to the water,' he later narrated. A jubilant Rommel had arrived at the English Channel.

A Luftwaffe (WL on the licence plate = Wehrmachtsteil Luftwaffe) Sd.Kfz. 223 Leichter Panzerspähwagen Funk crosses a canal bridge on 5 June. This vehicle was used by the Fliegerverbindungsoffizier (Flivo) – the flying liaison officer assigned to the 7th Panzer Division.

Writing with swagger, Alfred Tschimpke described a 'Storm over the Somme'. 'In the evening the Somme had been crossed in a wide strip and the first positions on the Weygand line had been broken through. It was thought to be even more impassable than the Maginot Line. One should be careful with high-sounding words!'

'The sight of the sea with cliffs either side was a thrill and a spur to each one of us,' Rommel rejoiced. 'We climbed out of vehicles and walked down the shingle beach to the water's edge, and let it lap against our boots.'

11 June 1940. The 25th Panzer Regiment advanced from Veulettes-sur-Mer east towards Saint-Valery en Caux, some 7 miles (11km) distant. Located at the mouth of the Durdent River, Veulettes has the longest seafront on the Côte d'Albâtre (Alabaster Coast), a stretch of coastline characterised by high chalk cliffs extending for 75 miles (120km) from La Hève Cape outside Le Havre at the mouth of the Seine, north-west to the village of Le Tréport.

Allied prisoners caught by the speed of the German advance. Captain Derek Lang, adjutant of the 4th Camerons, recalled how 'some of the troops had tried to descend the three-hundred-foot cliffs on ropes. Few could have succeeded judging by the smashed bodies lying on the beach, while a hundred and fifty feet above we could see the frayed ends of their broken ropes. Most appalling of all were the wounded. They were everywhere, and on our approach called out to us for water, or to help bind up their wounds.'

Rommel directed Hauptmann Hans von Luck to take an 8.8cm battery and secure Fécamp while he advanced on Saint-Valery. No opposition was encountered, and von Luck's troops reached the hills north of the town on the evening of 9 June. Undetected, they spotted two RN destroyers preparing for an evacuation. An emissary sent into the town the next morning brought news that while the mayor and French commander wished to surrender, the British were standing firm. With a repeat overture refused, the Germans threatened to shell the town at midday. A civilian waving a white cloth appeared at 11.30 a.m., pleading for the town to be spared. Shortly before noon, the destroyers steamed out of the harbour, shooting at the German positions. Entering the town, von Luck was presented with the key to the seaside resort by a grateful mayor, his town spared. Fécamp's war memorial, saluting its First World War heroes, was sculpted by François Sicard. It depicts a soldier and sailor in an act of brotherhood, holding hands.

Artillery on the heights east of Fécamp. In the foreground is a French 95mm gun model 1888, behind a German Model 30 2cm Flak 30 anti-aircraft gun.

View of the fishing village of Fécamp's harbour and the chapel Notre-Dame-du-Salut on the hill behind. Hans von Luck radioed Rommel that the town had been taken with light casualties (6 men), with 200 enemy soldiers taken prisoner. The French Navy was able to tow away a few sub-chasers under construction before the town fell.

The coastal resort of Étretat beach and the L'Aiguille creuse (hollow needle) pinnacle, some 10 miles (16km) south-west of Fécamp. The arrival of advance elements ruined plans for Allied divisions to withdraw along the coast and forced a rapid evacuation from Saint-Valery-en-Caux on 11 June.

Les Loges, route d'Étretat/route de Gonneville-la-Mallet, was protected by a 75mm gun (*canon de 75mm Mle 97 sur affut à crinoline*). The strongpoint was a part of the defensive line to protect Le Havre. The shop in the foreground is a grocery: *A l'alimentation – Liquides à emporter.*

The French Navy ship P21 *Cérons* left Cherbourg on 8 June 1940, bound for Le Havre. On the evening of 11 June, she received orders to sail to Saint-Valery-en-Caux with a flotilla of twenty or so ships – trawlers, fishing boats and patrol boats P22 *Sauternes* and P36 *Patrie*. Led by a British destroyer, the flotilla left Saint-Valery-en-Caux at 3.15 a.m. and arrived at Veules-les-Roses before 5.45 a.m. to evacuate BEF and French troops. P21 *Cérons* was lying at anchor 300 metres off Veules-les-Roses when small boats were launched to evacuate the surrounded Allied soldiers. Under attack, the flotilla returned fire. At 7.00 a.m., *Cérons*, with 300 troops on board, weighed anchor, only to run aground. Captain Eve ordered the transfer of the 300 men to P22 *Sauternes*. Hit by shellfire, Captain Lucien Eve, Enseigne de Vaisseau de 1ère classe de reserve (reserve lieutenant in the French Navy) ordered 'Abandon ship'. The remaining eighty-one men on board were landed on the beach. Still under German fire at 11.00 a.m, *Cérons'* stern was destroyed by the exploding depth charges. Eve and his remaining crewmen were taken prisoner around midday. Rommel described the encounter in his *Papers*: 'About 1,000 yards north-east of St Valery an enemy transport was just steaming out to sea. Our AA battery had ceased fire. I at once had fire reopened on the enemy transport from an 88mm gun close by, although the mounting of this gun had been hit and it no longer stood firmly on all four feet. The crew worked splendidly, and shells were soon falling hard by the ship. However, the damage to the mounting made it impossible to apply the necessary corrections. Meanwhile, the gun had come under fire from a British auxiliary cruiser lying 1,000 yards offshore. A smoke screen, which I had laid to cover the gun from the warship's fire, proved very effective. Our gun crew, however, had no success with the enemy transport. Dive-bombers had already been called up by radio. Shortly afterwards I met a forward observer from a 100mm battery and instructed him to take the enemy auxiliary cruiser under fire immediately. At 1040 hours the ship was set alight by several hits and beached by her crew.' Formerly a Worms shipping company freighter built in 1923, *Cérons* was converted into an armed merchantman in September 1939 and renamed P21. Armed with four 100mm guns, two 37mm anti-aircraft guns, six machine guns on four carriages, thirty-eight depth charges plus smoke apparatus, she had a crew of seventy-nine men (officers, petty officers and seamen). Two 100mm guns were salvaged in 1995 and installed in a memorial.

Visiting Le Havre on 9 June, British Admiral Sir William James directed his destroyers to investigate the disembarkation of troops from some of the smaller Normandy ports to the east. A mixed armada of 67 merchant ships and 140 smaller vessels would be employed to undertake another Dunkirk-like evacuation. The operation was originally planned for 10 June, but the British 51st Division had not yet arrived. Fate intervened through a combination of fog and heavy rain on the night of 11 June, delaying the operation at Saint-Valery-en-Caux, especially since only sixteen ships were equipped with radio and the army had few compatible sets. By 12 June, Rommel's guns commanded the western cliffs overlooking the town, where the men of the 51st Division had withdrawn. An evacuation undertaken at the eastern end of Veules-les-Roses, some 4 miles (6km) east, successfully rescued 2,137 British and 1,184 French troops under heavy shellfire.

Sainte-Marie-des-Champs/Écalles-Alix. A column of Pz.Kpfw. 38(t) tanks advance along road N14 (today D6015) from Barentin. German vehicles parked on the left include a Sd.Kfz. 223 armoured car, and a mittlerer Einheits-PKW (Kfz. 15). According to Rommel: 'At 0730 hours [10 June] I drove round the north of Rouen to Barentin, giving orders by radio on the way for the division to join up with me. Road demolitions were reported by the Reconnaissance Battalion east of Yvetot. They were also repeatedly reporting the capture of British prisoners both with and without vehicles. … I arrived at the road fork east of the town shortly before 1000 hours and the AA batteries came in one after the other a few minutes later. They went straight into position at top speed and received orders to lay down a heavy fire on the road, on which a large number of enemy vehicles could already be seen. When the Panzer Regiment appeared in sight of Yvetot at about 1030 hours, I had the Reconnaissance Battalion launched against the crossroad two miles east of Ourville, closely followed over the same road by the Panzer Regiment.'

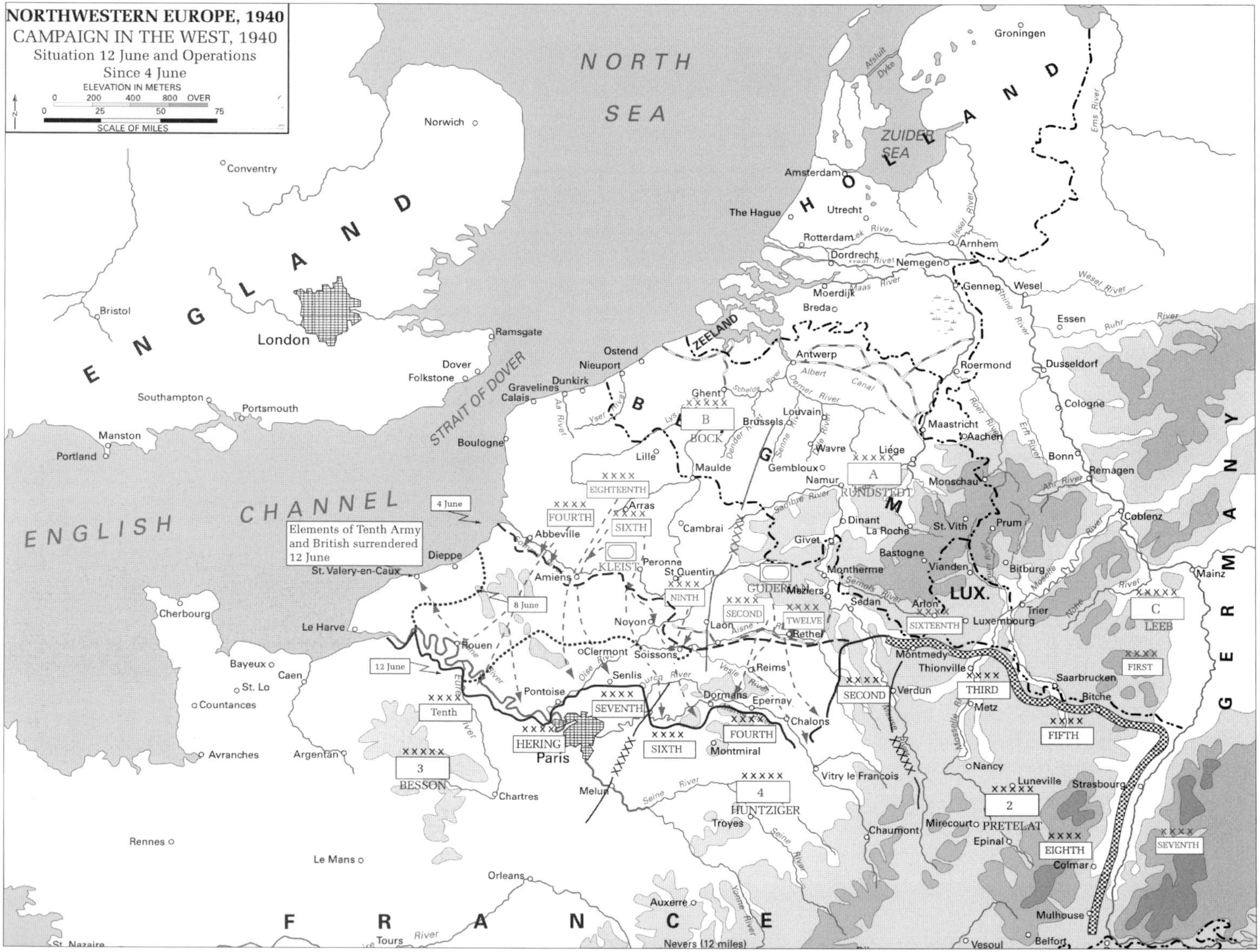
NORTHWESTERN EUROPE, 1940
CAMPAIGN IN THE WEST, 1940
Situation 12 June and Operations
Since 4 June
ELEVATION IN METERS
0 200 400 800 OVER
SCALE OF MILES
0 25 50 75
NORTH SEA
ENGLISH CHANNEL
STRAIT OF DOVER
ENGLAND
HOLLAND
ZUIDER SEA
ZEELAND
LUX.
FRANCE
GERMANY
Norwich
Coventry
Bristol
London
Ramsgate
Dover
Folkstone
Southampton
Portsmouth
Manston
Portland
Groningen
Amsterdam
The Hague
Utrecht
Rotterdam
Dordrecht
Nemegen
Arnhem
Moerdijk
Breda
Gennep
Wesel
Essen
Antwerp
Roermond
Dusseldorf
Cologne
Ostend
Nieuport
Dunkirk
Gravelines
Calais
Boulogne
Ghent
Brussels
Louvain
Maastricht
Aachen
Bonn
Remagen
Lille
Maulde
Wavre
Liége
Gembloux
Namur
Monschau
Coblenz
Mainz
Arras
Cambrai
Dinant
La Roche
St. Vith
Prum
Givet
Bastogne
Viandep
Bitburg
Abbeville
Amiens
Peronne
St Quentin
Montherme
Meziers
Sedan
Arlon
Trier
Luxembourg
Dieppe
St. Valery-en-Caux
Le Harve
Cherbourg
Rouen
Noyon
Laon
Rethel
Clermont
Soissons
Reims
Montmedy
Thionville
Saarbrucken
Bitche
Bayeux
Caen
St. Lo
Countances
Senlis
Pontoise
Dormans
Epernay
Chalons
Verdun
Metz
Avranches
Argentan
Paris
Melun
Montmiral
Nancy
Vitry le Francois
Luneville
Strasbourg
Chartres
Troyes
Chaumont
Mirecourt
Epinal
Colmar
Rennes
Le Mans
Orleans
Auxerre
Mulhouse
Belfort
Vesoul
Tours
St. Nazaire
Nevers (12 miles)
Ems River
Rhine River
Lek River
Maas River
Albert Canal
Demer River
Scheldt River
Lys
Yser
Aa River
Dender River
Senne River
Sambre River
Roer River
Erft River
Ahr River
Moselle River
Nahe
Semois River
Aisne
Oise River
Ourcq River
Vesle River
Meuse
Seine River
Yonne River
Eure River
4 June
8 June
12 June
Elements of Tenth Army and British surrendered 12 June
B BOCK
A RUNDSTEDT
C LEEB
EIGHTEENTH
FOURTH
SIXTH
KLEIST
NINTH
GUDERIAN
SECOND
TWELVE
SIXTEENTH
FIRST
Tenth
HERING
SEVENTH
FOURTH
SIXTH
SECOND
THIRD
FIFTH
3 BESSON
4 HUNTZIGER
2 PRETELAT
EIGHTH
SEVENTH

Louviers in ruins. Situated some 19 miles (30km) south-east of Rouen, Louviers, was bombed by the Luftwaffe on 9, 11 and 12 June 1940. The town became an inferno between 12 and 13 June, with 550 homes destroyed. This photograph was taken in Rue Maréchal Foch, an area devastated during the final day of bombing. The church in the background is Église Notre-Dame (built in the twelfth and thirteenth centuries and later modified in the fifteenth and sixteenth centuries). The German column is driving likely southward towards Évreux. Following the 1944 D-Day landings, the Allies liberated the town on 25 August. Louviers was later awarded the French *Croix de Guerre* (War Cross) on 26 June 1949, acknowledging the 1940 bombing, the retaliatory destruction by the occupying Germans and the deaths of ten notable residents who died after being deported.

11 June 1940. German armour pictured on the heights west of Saint-Valery-en-Caux. 'A hazy grey morning hangs over the coast,' Alfred Tschimpke recounted. 'It is of great use to the English. In the shelter of this natural fog, they try to save themselves on their ships and across to England.'

Two armoured command vehicles: Pz.Befehlswagen 38 (t), left, and Pz.Kpf.Wg. I. One of the British defenders, Angus Campbell (2nd Battalion, Seaforth Highlanders) was under heavy mortar in an apple orchard, about a mile from the coast, when the last order came – 'Every man for himself.' He described German tanks 'like sheepdogs herding us to the edge of the cliffs, which stood grim and steep, over two hundred feet high. On the bare tops there was no rock or outcrop you could crouch behind to defend yourself. When it was clear there was no way out they closed in and ordered us to throw down our arms and surrender. Our war was over.'

Hands aloft and white flags. Allied servicemen surrender on the heights above Saint-Valery. The day before, Mussolini had 'stabbed his neighbour in the back' by declaring war on France; four days later, German troops entered Paris. Many Allied troops descended the cliffs (in the rear) using improvised ropes fashioned from blankets and rifle slings. With Dieppe surrounded and the road to Le Havre blocked, the fate of the 51st (Highland) Division was sealed. General Victor Fortune directed the remainder of his division to fall back and establish perimeter defences around the town.

Future absconder. The British naval officer pictured above is Commander Robert Elkins, Naval Liaison Officer with the 51st (Highland) Division. Escaping on 15 June, Elkins returned home to England on a commandeered sailboat. A midshipman wrote: 'On 18th July [1940] we got a new Commander, one R.F. Elkins. … Elkins gave a talk about his expedition to St Valery to embark the 51st Highland Division. Alas, as history relates, he arrived just before the German army cut off the 51st from the harbour. He soon found the German army peering down on the harbour from the cliff tops, and he opened fire on the Wehrmacht with a .303 rifle. They told him not to be silly as they could soon blow him out, and up, and demanded his surrender. He therefore obliged, but some days later managed to give them the slip and marched westward until he came to an as yet uncaptured small harbour. He then pinched a boat and sailed back home.' Rommel later wrote of a 'naval officer who had spent a long time haranguing his men on the mole and apparently succeeded in dissuading them from surrendering. Finally, we opened up on this officer with machine-guns. … For half an hour he lay as if dead behind a heap of stones, but then decided it was better to surrender.' Accused by Johannes Schräpler as the cause of unnecessary casualties, Elkins replied: 'Would you have acted differently in my situation?'

'More and more prisoners are climbing from St Valery,' states the original caption scrawled on the back of the photograph.

Meanwhile, the defending troops in the town began building barricades in preparation for the German attack.

Clifftop captives. On the evening of 11 June, Rommel sent several German-speaking prisoners into the town, still full of Allied troops, with an ultimatum to surrender by 9 p.m. Marched under white flags to the hills west of the town, the negotiating troops returned having failed to achieve an outcome. In the belief that the British were attempting an embarkation, 'the concentrated fire of the division was let loose', Rommel chronicled. 'A Pz.Kpfw. IV crashed through the heavy barricade on the pier, where there were numerous guns, and set it aflame. Fires soon raged everywhere.' Nonetheless, the 'tenacious' British refused to surrender.

Allied troops – Rommel noted: '1,000 prisoners' – with their backs to the sea above the Saint-Valery lighthouse.

'Heavy artillery fire on St Valery shall make the occupation troops ready to surrender,' recorded Rommel on the reverse of the original photograph. On 9 June, British Admiral Sir William James visited Le Havre and directed his destroyers to investigate the disembarkation of troops from some of the smaller Normandy ports to the east. A mixed armada of sixty-seven merchant ships and 140 smaller vessels would be employed to undertake another Dunkirk-like evacuation. The operation was originally planned for 10 June but the division had not yet arrived. Fate intervened and a combination of fog and heavy rain on the night of 11 June delayed the operation at Saint-Valery-en-Caux, especially since only sixteen ships were equipped with radio and the army had few compatible sets. By 12 June, Rommel's guns commanded the western cliffs overlooking the town, where the men of the 51st Division had withdrawn. An evacuation undertaken at the eastern end of Veules-les-Roses, some 4 miles (6km) east, successfully rescued 2,137 British and 1,184 French troops under heavy shellfire.

12 June 1940. 'St Valery. After capturing the hilltop, they are listening to the first special announcement about the battle that has been won.'

A 'well-deserved lunch break after the battle on the heights above St Valery was won'. The soft-skin vehicles include (left to right) an Opel Blitz 3-ton, Leichter Einheits-PKW and Mercedes Benz type 200 Cabriolet.

Trapped in the small littoral town, Gregor Macdonald of the Cameron Highlanders described the increasingly desperate situation:

> Every square foot was occupied by troops, some dead, but asleep in the torrential rain which had started at dusk. To make matters worse, fog was rolling in from the sea and there was no sign of any Royal Navy ships. A steady concentration of shellfire was coming from a south-westerly direction. ... Stretcher-bearers were carrying bodies to the town square where a huge heap was steadily growing.

12 June 1940. 'The coast and St Valery ablaze.'

Scenes of surrender inside St Valery; stills from a German newsreel.

Rommel recorded the devastating effect of his division's fire on the northern part of the town.

A miscellany of equipment, including a 40mm Bofors anti-aircraft gun, abandoned by the BEF.

An upturned 40mm Bofors anti-aircraft gun, the standard light anti-aircraft gun of the British Army, and a Bedford type MWD.

In a scene reminiscent of Rommel's earlier arrival at Les Petites-Dalles, a Pz.Kpfw. II symbolically reaches the water's edge.

Abandoned BEF trucks (left to right): an Austin Type K 2, Austin K 3 and Bedford OYD. In the foreground is a Pz.Kpfw. II.

Smouldering buildings line the Saint-Valery seafront along L'Esplanade, adjacent to the *nouvelle digue-promenade* (new seawall). The burning half-timbered house in the left foreground is the Grand hôtel de la plage et du casino, the west cliff providing the backdrop.

Note the Kriegsmarine sailor (left) and two Pz.Kpfw. 38 (t) tanks on L'Esplanade.

German armoured cars advance along Route de Dieppe from Saint-Valery-en-Caux harbour. The street on the right is Rue Nationale. The abandoned truck is a British Bedford OYD general-service (GS) cargo vehicle.

Place de l´Hôtel de Ville – Saint-Valery's town square. The building with the damaged roof (right) was the city hall. Barricading British vehicles, a Universal Carrier and Bedford trucks, stretch across the square. The sign reads: *Circulation Déviée – Tourner le Bassin – Fécamp* (Detour/diversion – Drive around the basin [of the port] to Fécamp).

German vehicles pictured in the town square include an 8.5-ton Sd.Kfz. 251/6 mittlerer Kommandopanzerwagen Ausf A and Einheitsdiesel 6 x 6 truck.

Another view of the recently occupied place de l'Hôtel de Ville. Rommel: 'I followed the infantry across a narrow bridge to the square. The town hall, and many buildings all around were either burnt out or still ablaze. Barricades constructed by the enemy from vehicles and guns, also showed the effect of our barrage.'

'British and French troops were now pouring into the square from all directions,' Rommel narrated, 'where they formed up in column and marched off west.' Note the Universal Carrier and Ordnance QF 2-pounder anti-tank guns. Captured 2-pounders entered German service as the 4.0cm Pak 192 (e). The weapon was hindered in combat by its high silhouette and the lack of a high-explosive shell.

More views of the place de l'Hôtel de Ville and the makeshift Allied barricade. Rommel's casualties during the fighting at Saint-Valery on 11–12 June were forty-seven men killed and seventy-one wounded.

Looking towards Saint-Valery's *avant-port* (outer harbour), left to right: the *quai d'Aval* (downstream dock), the *avant-port* and the *quai d'Amont* (upstream dock). The small tidal harbour was inaccessible to shipping at low tide. In the background left, the last house of the *quai d'Aval* is the villa Cap-Trompette, which still stands today. The burning houses along the Rue des Frères Leloutre, right, were destroyed during the war.

Another photo looking along the harbour basin. Alfred Tschimpke noted: 'Brown uniforms are visible, faces with domed and flat steel helmets, raised hands. Prisoners. … Before us lies the wide lock basin, it is almost waterless. A narrow bridge leads over to the other side. Over there, all the houses are shot up. Behind them is the quay. From there heavy machine fire still hammers.'

Major General Victor Fortune, commanding officer of the 51st (Highland) Division, 'waited all night' for an evacuation, ultimately thwarted by fog. There would be no repeat of Dunkirk. Fortune was shocked to find a white flag flying above a church steeple on the morning of 12 June. Demanding that it be removed, he was disappointed to learn from a Frenchman that Général Marcel Ihler had already surrendered. A note received shortly afterwards from another French soldier advised that '9 Corps will cease fire at 8 a.m.'. Fortune responded with a message to the War Office: 'I have been ordered to cease fire from 0800 by Comdt Ninth Corps. I am in the process of trying to clear enemy machine guns from cliffs overlooking the harbour. A difficult situation exists in St Valery as all French elements have ceased fire … [and] hanging out white flags. I have informed Corps Comdt. that my policy is that I cannot, repeat cannot, comply with his orders until I am satisfied that there is no possibility of evacuating by boat any of my division later.' Just over two hours later, a 51st Division signalman was present when Fortune was forced to reconsider his position: 'Just then enemy shells started whizzing over the top of the small house we were in. They seemed to come nearer and nearer until it sounded as if they were just missing the chimney pots. With an anguish which I will never forget, the General decided that he had little option but to obey the orders, and he said: "Tell someone to hoist the bloody flag on the church tower."' Tschimpke waxed lyrical on the meeting of victor and vanquished. 'Now they face each other. On the one side the German general, the man with the *Pour le Mérite* and the Knight's Cross, the commander of the legendary "Ghost Division", with the taut, tanned soldier's face. On the other side, the long, gray-haired English general. For the first time they see each other face-to-face, these two divisional commanders who have been crossing blades for 14 days. One of them attacker and reckless daredevil from the first day of the campaign. The other pursued, always in retreat, repeatedly beaten again. And now, hard on the coast, which could mean both rescue or demise, he has the fate of captivity. They examine each other with weighing eyes. No muscle twitches in both faces. The Englishman goes to the Germans. Silently, both put their hands on the cap edge. Then the English general receives the instructions for the removal of his troops into captivity.'

Rommel: 'During the next few hours no less than twelve generals were brought in as prisoners, among them four divisional commanders. A particular joy for us was the inclusion among them of General Fortune.'

Général Marcel Ihler's aide-de-camp explained to Rommel that four French and one British division would surrender. In the coming hours, twelve generals were brought in as prisoners, including Jacques Chanoine, Arsène Vauthier (right with cigarette), André Durand and Paul Gastey. Rommel was no doubt pleased to hear the complaint from one general that he was 'too fast, much too fast for us. That's all there is to it.'

General Fortune's senior staff officer, Lieutenant Colonel Henry Swinburn, later wrote of a dejected-looking Général Marcel Ihler (wearing *képi*) arriving at Fortune's headquarters at La Chaussée, roughly 7 miles south of Dieppe, to report that his entire corps, including the 51st Division, was doomed. German troops had entered Rouen, cutting off the French commander from the town to which he had been ordered to retreat. Ihler and Fortune remained prisoners until 1945.

Rommel (with camera) and Général Marcel Ihler outside the former Hôtel de la Paix. Alfred Tschimpke recorded that Ihler, 'an old, tired man, drove up to the market square in a long, black limousine [a Peugeot type 402] with some of his staff officers.'

'The commanding general of the French IX Corps surrenders.' Rommel continued: 'Shortly afterwards an NCO reported to me that a high ranking French general had been taken prisoner on the eastern side of the town and was asking to see me. A few minutes later the French General Ihler [facing Rommel] came up to me wearing an unmarked military trench coat. His escort officer fell to the rear as he approached. When I asked the General what division he commanded, he replied in broken German: "No Division. I command IX Corps."'

Generalmajor Ludwig Crüwell (right), commander of the 5th Panzer Division from 6 June to 4 July 1940, would serve under Rommel on 31 July 1941, when he was appointed commander of the Afrika Korps while Rommel assumed command of Panzer Army Afrika. Fate later intervened while Crüwell was inspecting operations by air on 29 May 1942. His pilot mistook British soldiers for Italians and landed, whereupon he was taken prisoner.

Rommel and Ihler. In April the following year, as German armoured columns neared the Libyan port of Tobruk, Rommel directed his Panzer commander, General Johannes Streich, to attack 'with everything we have … before Tommy has time to dig in'. Perhaps Rommel sensed an opportunity to emulate his victory at Saint-Valery.

Major Joachim Ziegler, Ic Dritter Generalstabsoffizier (Chief Intelligence Officer) (left), confers with Général de division Arsène Vauthier. Ziegler, a veteran of the Condor Legion in Spain, served as Rommel's intelligence officer in France. Later transferred to the Waffen-SS, in 1944 he was promoted *to* SS-Brigadeführer und Generalmajor der Waffen-SS and commander of the SS Division Nordland. He died in the fighting for Berlin on 2 May 1945.

The ignominy of surrender. Left to right: Major Joachim Ziegler; Generalmajor Erwin Rommel; Major iG Otto Heidkämper; Oberst Georg von Bismarck, face obscured by Général de corps Marcel Ihler (with back to camera); an army interpreter; a newly liberated Luftwaffe pilot; Leutnant der Reserve Karl Hanke (hands on hips); and Major General Victor Fortune. During the final assault on the town, Rommel had assigned a Panzer company to the ill-qualified Hanke, who panicked after a shell splinter jammed the turret on his tank, halting the advance until Oberst Karl Rothenburg's adjutant intervened.

The bareheaded Luftwaffe pilot (left) was shot down several days earlier at Rouen and taken prisoner. Now responsible for guarding the senior Allied prisoners, he was, Rommel noted, 'visibly delighted' by his new assignment, relishing 'the role reversal'. Leutnant Alfred Tschimpke noted that Ihler had earlier 'instructed the captured German Luftwaffe lieutenant, who is now standing at the side of the German general, to go to the Germans as a *parlementaire*, accompanied by French soldiers with white flags. But he had only reached as far as the English line before rifle fire turned him back. So while the French soldiers were already smashing their rifles, the English still wanted to continue their completely hopeless resistance until their last man was evacuated by sea. The evening before, the French commanding general complained to the Luftwaffe officer of his sorrow, venting his displeasure at the unreasonable behaviour of the English.'

Another surrender image (note the photographer in the background). Joseph Goebbels, head of the Reichsministerium für Volksaufklärung und Propaganda (Reich Ministry for Popular Enlightenment and Propaganda) urged the 10 per cent of Germans – some 7 million people – who owned a camera in 1939 to continue their craft in wartime. The magazine *Photofreund* similarly reminded the swelling ranks of amateur photographers in uniform that 'it is the unconditional duty of every soldier to keep his camera in action'. The German High Command invited soldiers to create a unique souvenir of their 'special war experiences'. To capture and share their military service, many soldiers marched off to war carrying private 35mm, 127 or 120 format cameras in their field packs. Their snapshots, the German film manufacturer Agfa advertised, would provide a 'bridge between the Front and Home'. The sheer number of private photographs taken in war was unprecedented, the majority in France and Russia. 'It seems funny,' US journalist William L. Shirer observed in occupied Paris in June 1940, 'but every German soldier carries a camera. I saw by the thousand today photographing Notre-Dame, the Arc de Triomphe, the Invalides.' Many pictures, Shirer noted, were naturally of a sightseer nature snapped by amateur photographers.

Striking a victorious pose beside Fortune and his senior staff officer, Lieutenant Colonel Henry Swinburn (second from right). Rommel and his party were 'particularly struck by the *sangfroid* [composure] with which the British officers met their fate. The general, and his staff officers in particular, strolled around the street in front of the house laughing. The only thing that seemed to irritate them was the constant photography they had to suffer at the hands of our Propaganda Company and other photographers.' Swinburn had earlier noted in his war diary: 'The activities of the 51st Highland Division ceased.'

'The battle is over here.' Writing home to his wife, Rommel boasted of capturing one corps and four divisional commanders; 'Wonderful moments!' Allied resistance at Saint-Valery did, however, permit the evacuation of troops from Le Havre with only interference from the Luftwaffe.

Rommel, Hanke and Ziegler (centre, left to right) confer. The distinctive Condor Legion Tank Combat Badge displayed by Joachim Ziegler was one of four combat qualification badges that could be worn on the left breast pocket. The other three awards were the Infantry Assault Badge, the Tank Combat Badge and the Engineers' Assault Badge, which later became the General Assault Badge.

Victory luncheon. Alfred Tschimpke described a scene where Rommel and his senior officers were served a meal of peas with bacon, a 'goulash cannon' (a slang term for field kitchen) gala dinner. In the background, a loudspeaker car broadcasts *Tafelmusik* (literally, table music), a term for a type of sixteenth-century music played at a feast or banquet. Rommel noted that the captured generals were also invited to dine but politely declined. 'We ate alone.'

'Leftovers' from the Englishmen. Left to right: Austin Type K 2 and Bedford type MWD. The German soldier on the left shoulders an MG 34 machine gun on a bipod. Note the Esso petrol pump. Exxon launched Esso super grade fuel in France, Germany and Italy in 1929.

Rommel beside his assigned command vehicle, a Sd.Kfz. 263 (8-Rad) Funkspähwagen.

'Following the tanks came battalions of infantry,' Gregor Macdonald of the Cameron Highlanders recounted, '… with many of the officers speaking fluent English. Without fuss they instructed us to place our rifles and bayonets in one pile and the remainder of our equipment on a grassy bank above the road.'

Saint-Valery. View of *basin à flot* from *quai du Havre*: (left to right) the *écluse de navigation* (ship lock, single gate) with a footbridge, the *écluses de chasse* (flush locks) and the place de l'hôtel de ville in the background. The building on the left is the former Hôtel de la Paix, used in 1940 as Patronage des écoles publiques de la ville de Rouen – Colonie de vacances à la mer (Rouen state schools youth club – a children's holiday seaside camp).

Viewed from the opposite direction, Allied prisoners cross the wooden footbridge across the *écluse de navigation* (ship lock).

Prisoner from the 51st (Highland) Division, Donald MacDonald recalled: 'None of those present could comprehend fully the implications of these words. Not a man standing there had considered in his heart such an eventuality. No one had any inkling or insight that most of the British army was already in England, having been evacuated from Dunkirk. So, therefore, surprise was the first emotion that affected our minds. But, as the major continued to speak, the facts began to sink in and we realised the situation was not just dangerous but completely without hope. The enemy that surrounded us had vastly superior numbers and firepower and there was no way that a boat could get within a mile of the shore. The battle had been fought and the battle had been lost.'

Rommel found it 'impossible to estimate the total count of prisoners and booty. Some 12,000 men, of whom 8,000 were British, were carried off by the 7th Panzer Division's vehicles alone. The total number captured at St Valery is reputed to have numbered 46,000 men.' The British Highland Division was subsequently reformed and later served with honour across North Africa, Italy, France-liberating Saint-Valery – and, finally, in the defeat of Germany.

The battle over, 'the first inhabitants are coming back'. Former General Siegfried Westphal believed that the relations between German soldiers and the French 'were extremely gratifying at this time, and remained good for some while. It appeared that the "hereditary enmity" between the French and German peoples no longer existed. It was only after the agents of [Heinrich] Himmler, [Fritz] Sauckel and [Alfred] Rosenberg on the other that a mutual estrangement inevitably set in.'

German tanks 'guard the Channel coast'. Sir John Colville, Churchill's secretary, noted in his diary that Saint-Valery was the 'most brutal disaster which we have yet suffered'. Churchill later recounted how the 'greater part of the 51st Division, with many of the French, was cut off. It was a case of gross mismanagement for this very danger was visible a full three days before.' Today a granite memorial to the 51st (Highland) Division overlooks the town. An inscription reads: 'IN PROUD AND GRATEFUL MEMORY OF ALL RANKS OF THE 51st (HIGHLAND) DIVISION WHO GAVE THEIR LIVES DURING THE WAR 1939–45 LÀ A' BHLÀIR 'S MATH NA CÀIRDEAN [ON THE DAY OF BATTLE IT IS GOOD TO HAVE FRIENDS].'

'Dearest Lu,' Rommel penned in a letter to his wife on 12 June. 'The battle is over here. Today one corps commander and four division commanders presented themselves before me in the market square of St Valery, having been forced by my division to surrender. Wonderful moments!'. As Rommel celebrated, Heinz Guderian smashed through the French line at Châlons-sur-Marne on 12 June, opening a gap between two French armies. Watching closely, Hitler was keen for concrete signs of collapse to garner political advantage and demonstrate to the world that French resistance was broken. Via the American ambassador, Berlin learned on 13 June that the French government had declared Paris an open city. German troops entered the following morning. Guderian reached the Swiss frontier three days later, trapping some 500,000 French troops within the Maginot Line. With France's fate sealed, the new French government under Marshal Philippe Pétain requested an armistice.

Marshal Philippe Pétain in his office as Vice President of the Council, in May 1940.

Chapter Three

'Le Havre is Taken'

The Allies clung to hopes of continued resistance. The day after Saint-Valery surrendered (13 June), British General Sir Alan Brooke arrived at Cherbourg, France's most important deep-water port. Evacuated from Dunkirk, Brooke returned to France on orders from the British War Cabinet to organise a new BEF. With a considerable number of British troops still in the field south of the Seine, reinforcements were to be shipped to Cherbourg and placed under General Maxime Weygand's command. The leading brigade of Britain's 52nd (Lowland) Division had already arrived. Other formations, including the 1st Canadian Division and the British 3rd Division, were to follow. The 7th Panzer Division, meanwhile, was directed to occupy Cherbourg as quickly as possible, the reasoning twofold: firstly, to prevent Allied forces regrouping in Brittany; secondly, Pétain's announcement of a ceasefire added an impetus for further German conquests and a stronger hand at the coming negotiating table.

'On to Le Havre,' Rommel penned on 14 June, 'it all went without bloodshed. We're now engaging targets out to sea with long-range artillery.'

Looking south from Cap de la Hève towards Le Havre. Visible in the distance is TSS *Bruges* (2,949 tons), a passenger ferry built by John Brown of Clydebank for Britain's Great Eastern Railway. Launched in March 1920, the ship was acquired by the London and North Eastern Railway in 1923 and placed on the Harwich to Antwerp route. Requisitioned as a troop transport, she was crippled in an attack by Luftwaffe aircraft 2 nautical miles off the coast, between Cauville and Saint-Jouin-Bruneval on the afternoon of 11 June 1940. At 1515 hours, marine pilot Émile Prentout, together with *Bruges'* captain, decided to save the crippled vessel by bringing her to Le Havre harbour. Wounded personnel were transferred by the motorboat *Sénateur-Louis-Brindeau* to the hospital carrier HMHS *Worthing*. With the ship taking on water it was decided at 1700 hours to beach her in front of Palais des Régates to prevent her from sinking. The wreck was later used for target practice by German artillery.

A battery of Canon de 240 TR Mle 1903 coastal artillery at Cap de la Hève, with its two distinctive lighthouses, outside Le Havre.

In 1940, the Canon de 240 TR Mle 1903 was the most modern French pre-WWI heavy coastal defence gun. Four were installed at Le Havre and Cherbourg. German occupying forces later installed four 15.5cm K. 418 (f) guns at Cap de la Hève.

An abandoned Vickers QF 3.7-inch Mk II AA gun is examined at Cap de la Hève. The French Army received twenty of these guns in 1940. Captured examples in Wehrmacht service were known as the 9.4cm Flak M. 39 (e).

Approaching Le Havre, smoke rising in the distance from burning oil tanks.

Driving south along the seafront at Sainte-Adresse towards Le Havre. On 9 June, Admiral Sir William James, Commander-in-Chief, Portsmouth, was ordered to arrange the evacuation of Allied troops from Le Havre in an operation codenamed 'Cycle'. An assortment of ships, including British and Canadian destroyers, a New Zealand sloop and support ships led by HMS *Codrington*, was dispatched to the French port. The flotilla arrived to find the port severely damaged by Luftwaffe bombing. Naval beach parties landed on 10 June and after a twenty-four-hour delay, the evacuation commenced the next day. Hampered by damage to the port, the embarkation proceeded smoothly aside from the attack on the requisitioned troopship SS *Bruges*, which was hit and beached. The evacuation was completed by dawn on 13 June, rescuing 11,059 British troops, 9,000 of whom were taken to Cherbourg.

A stop outside the Hôtel Nice Havrais, on Place Fréderic Sauvage, outside Le Havre. The assortment of vehicles includes a mittlerer Einheits-PKW (Kfz. 15), Sd.Kfz. 223 armoured car, a Ford (possibly type V8) and a Mercedes-Benz 170 VK. The motorcycle in front of the Ford is a BMW type R12. Note the swastikas, an aid for aerial recognition, prominently painted on the bonnets of several vehicles.

15 June 1940. Entering Le Havre, a Sd.Kfz. 10 halftrack and trailer and two Sd.Kfz. 222 armoured cars pause by the sea; TSS *Bruges* is beached in the background.

A German Schwere 10cm Kanone K 18 points out to sea. Ironically, the design flaws in the gun saw it phased out of service and relegated to coastal artillery. Rommel: 'On to Le Havre and inspected the town. It all went without bloodshed. We're now engaging targets out to sea with long-range artillery. Already one transport alight to-day.' Luftwaffe bombs had earlier sunk six transports at Le Havre. One ship, the *Niobé*, was loaded with ammunition intended for Dunkirk and was evacuating refugees when it received a direct hit. Only eleven people survived the massive explosion, which killed 800 soldiers, sailors, women, children and workers.

15 June 1940. Le Havre, Rue Magellan. Captioned: 'Traces of the "victorious retreat" of the Englishmen from Le Havre.' The mixed array of British trucks in the foreground includes two Bedford type MWD trucks, possibly a Morris-Commercial type CDF (far right), plus a Morris-Commercial C8 Quad field artillery tractor (centre). The building on the right is Le Havre station, housing administrative services. Designed in Art Deco style by architect Henry Pacon, it was built in 1932.

Above: More abandoned BEF vehicles. On the left, a mixture of Bedford OYD and OXD trucks. This photo is looking towards the Monument de la reconnaissance belge à la France, Le Havre and Sainte-Adresse on Boulevard de Strasbourg. The large bronze memorial was presented by Belgium in 1924 in recognition of services rendered by the city during the First World War. The monument was later hidden to prevent it being melted down and reused in Germany's armaments industry.

Le Havre. This is Place de l'Hôtel-de-ville at the intersection of Boulevard de Strasbourg on the left. (Note the sign pointing in the direction of the railway station, Harfleur and Rouen, via Boulevard de Strasbourg.) In the foreground on the left is Lloyds and National Provincial Foreign Bank (22, Place de l'Hôtel-de-ville in 1939); the building with arches in the background right is Comptoir national d'escompte de Paris (2, Rue Jules-Siegfried in 1939). This area was later destroyed by an RAF Bomber Command raid on 5 September 1944. The mix of vehicles (from left to right) includes a Morris-Commercial type CD, a limber (possibly a British 18-pdr field gun), a field artillery tractor (FAT) Morris-Commercial type C 8, a Bedford OXD or OYD, and a captured French Fiat type 626 N (one of 1,650 trucks ordered by France, of which some 700 had been delivered prior to the Italian declaration of war on 10 June 1940).

'Le Havre is taken,' Tschimpke elatedly wrote.

> Now only the two protruding coastal noses remain: Cherbourg and Brest. We're on our way to Cherbourg. A Kradschützenkompanie (armed motorcycle company) goes first. We drive through the oppressive warmth of the sun on a hot June day. … Even though we haven't had a good night's rest for two days, we haven't heard much gunfire aside from the bombs dropped by British aircraft, which missed our river bridges and hit neighbouring farmland.

A Kübelwagen later approached, an officer in the car calls out loudly:

> 'The French government is asking for a ceasefire!' … For a moment we lie frozen. It is instinctive to look at the time. It's 5:15 p.m. Gradually we become aware of the incomprehensible, the seriousness of this news. … For a moment, the shooters take their hands off the rifle they are holding. Armistice? Well, it will soon stop here. You pull your steel helmet off your forehead a little, it's easier to think when it's cool. … Faces remain turned toward the enemy, as befits soldiers in the field. It's still war here, in all its bloody seriousness.

Crossing the Seine

After a brief rest and time to reorganise, the 7th Panzer Division crossed the Seine at Poses on 16 June. The 7th Panzer Division resumed its advance to the French naval port of Cherbourg, encountering little resistance. 'We now came across small groups of French troops all along the route, who we had no difficulty in making our prisoners,' Rommel wrote. His motorcyclists happened upon a French column, taking it by surprise, though it 'did not seem very anxious to fight'. A French officer informed Rommel of Marshal Pétain's call for an armistice. Through an interpreter, Rommel advised that he knew nothing of the settlement; his orders were to keep marching. Instructing that his troops would not fire on surrendered troops, he called for the enemy column to move off the road and allow his vehicles to pass. 'We met more French troops behind this column and beckoned to them with white handkerchiefs,' Rommel continued, 'calling out that the war was over for them.'

Following a short pause, the armoured cars of the 37th Armoured Reconnaissance Battalion (now under Leutnant Isermayer after Major Günther Erdmann's earlier death) continued to advance via Flers. Waving to French troops on either side of the road, 'they stared in wonderment' as the German vehicles sped past. Approaching the outskirts of the town, a civilian with revolver drawn ran towards Rommel's car before French troops intervened and 'pulled him up short and prevented him carrying out his purpose'. Again, Rommel escaped harm. Impatient to reach the port, 'one French town after another was left behind us without a shot being fired,' he recounted. Encountering a staunchly defended roadblock, 'the leading vehicles were hit and three went up in flames.' Isermayer, in the first car, was 'seriously wounded in the head and lay unconscious beside his burning vehicle'. Rommel ordered the war-weary battalion, minus tanks or artillery, to break off until dawn. Since morning, the battalion had covered more than 150 miles – a milestone in

Barrage de Poses. Looking towards the Seine's right bank and the locks at Poses.

military history for a single day's advance, according to British military historian and pre-war advocate of armoured warfare Sir Basil Liddell Hart. 'In this war the commander's place is here, right out in the front!' Rommel had earlier told Oberst Kurt Hesse:

> I don't believe in armchair strategy. Let's leave that to the gentlemen of the General Staff. This is the age of [Prussian General Friedrich Wilhelm, baron von] Seydlitz and [General Hans Joachim von] Ziethen all over again. We've got to look at this war like a cavalry action – we've got to throw in tank divisions like cavalry squadrons, and that means issuing orders from a moving tank just as generals once used to from the saddle.

Abandoned British Army trucks outside Cherbourg form a makeshift roadblock. The vehicle in front on the right is a Bedford WT-series. The truck in the centre of the road is a Commer type Q 4.

Approaching Saint-Sauveur-le-Vicomte on 18 June 1940, Rommel's troops encountered obstacles left by retreating Allied troops. 'Baulks of timber', the general logged, 'had to be dragged out of the railings on either side of the bridge, where they had been anchored with heavy chains.' Engineers were also employed to remove a 100-yard-long barricade constructed from felled poplar trees (almost four years later, Rommel would be called upon to defend this same territory).

Pz.Kpfw. IV Ausf. D, the 'workhorse' of the Panzerwaffe; location unknown. Paul Henkelmann, a former Panzer driver, recalled the 150-mile (241km) advance from the Seine to the Cotentin Peninsula in a single day: 'The only real constraints on our advance were the wear and tear on our vehicles. The mobile workshops were kept extremely busy, but the weather was good and we knew that the end of the campaign was in sight. I personally felt that we had just won the war.'

In the aftermath of the fall of Paris and Verdun (scene of one of the bloodiest First World War battles) and a breakthrough in the Maginot Line near Saarbrücken, Rommel observed how the 'war seems to be gradually becoming a more or less peaceful occupation of all France. The population is peacefully disposed, and in some places very friendly.'

With unrestrained rhetoric, an officer who formerly served with Rommel in the First World War wrote: 'His magic word is speed. Boldness is his stock-in-trade. He shocks the enemy, takes them unawares, outflanks them. … Thus his tanks carve long, bloodstained trails across the map of Europe like the scalpel of a surgeon.'

Chapter Four

Swastika over Cherbourg

Harbouring doubts about a new continental 'redoubt' – the 'Brittany plan'– into which French troops would retreat, and from where the French government might take refuge, General Alan Brooke informed Anthony Eden, Britain's Secretary for War, that his mission had 'no military value and no hope of success'. Brooke pressed Churchill to evacuate all of the remaining British troops from France. Initially standing firm, the British prime minister relented, sanctioning the evacuation of roughly 200,000 British and Allied troops from ports in north-western France. As noted earlier, Pétain had requested an armistice on 17 June. Admiral Jean Louis Xavier François Darlan, however, ordered that the fight must continue since negotiations were yet to be finalised. He also directed the evacuation of Cherbourg and other Atlantic coast harbours to begin that night. Luftwaffe reconnaissance, Rommel noted, 'had reported the presence in Cherbourg of either warships or transports', with embarkation likely. The 7th Panzer Division's drive on Cherbourg continued under the harassing fire of warships positioned on either side of the Cotentin Peninsula. Several defensive positions outside the city also stymied the German advance. Approaching the port, Rommel noted 'several anti-aircraft balloons hanging in the sky over the port'. Shortly afterwards, the guns of the French forts opened fire. 'Everyone dived for cover,' Rommel narrated. 'The situation which had appeared to be going so well, took a sudden turn against us before 4 p.m., when, within a few minutes of each other, many of Cherbourg's forts opened a tremendous barrage.'

'We are on a gentle rise above Cherbourg,' Alfred Tschimpke detailed.

> The city is deserted. The population met us on the march here in long trains of refugees. On all these dusty, bitter faces lay the silent questioning of the why of such a fate. … From the forts far out protecting the approach to the harbour, the glare of the muzzle flashes of the heavy shore batteries flashed incessantly. The air is filled with the vibrations of the heavy impacts. Exploiting every cover in this hilly meadow terrain, the German riflemen wound their way closer and closer to the town. … The shells of the heavy German batteries whizzed overhead with a rattling noise. Blow after blow. Layer after layer hammers into the fortifications. But always new enemy machine gun nests make themselves felt. Bursts of fire are sprayed at the attackers

from ever new directions. … Stuka dive-bombing is ordered. The aircraft prepare to attack. The air rumbles with the roar of the engines. In a sudden nosedive, one after another of the machines drop down from above. You see the bombs falling, and a little later the whole wide area of the valley basin trembles with the concussive blast of explosions. Huge clouds of smoke, black and menacing, have risen. … Cherbourg will fall, one way or the other.

Across the Channel, Winston Churchill delivered one of his finest speeches: 'What General Weygand calls the "Battle of France" is over. The Battle of Britain is about is begin. … Hitler knows that he will have to break us in this island, or lose the war.'

Rommel drove forward towards Cherbourg before 6 a.m. on the morning of 19 June. Surrender leaflets printed in French were given to prisoners sent into Cherbourg, the general impatient for the port to capitulate.

Rommel's divisional staff gather at the end of Rue del la Paix in Équeurdreville, west of Cherbourg on the Normandy coast.

Driving through Cherbourg towards the Gare Maritime Transatlantique railway station. The building in the middle of the photo with a small turret on the top of the roof is a part of Cherbourg casino. Montagne du Roule provides the backdrop, with the coastal defences of Fort du Roule on top.

Cherbourg and the Gare Maritime (port railway station), right. Cherbourg became an important port in the nineteenth century after a series of artificial breakwaters and jetties were constructed to shield the harbour from severe weather. By the turn of the century, it had become an important international passenger hub for transatlantic liners. With the completion of the rail link in 1933, Cherbourg became the premier French passenger port of the period. Despite protests from the city's mayor, Vice Admiral Jules Le Bigot ordered many of the harbour installations to be destroyed.

Abandoned British transport, mostly Bedford OYD 3-ton trucks. The BEF's material losses were enormous – some 85,000 vehicles, 2,472 artillery pieces and hundreds of thousands of tons of munitions and stores. The final evacuation of troops from France, Operation Aerial, described by one historian as 'Churchill's second miracle of deliverance', began on 15 June. Nearly 186,000 troops – almost half the Dunkirk total – were rescued from Cherbourg, Granville, Saint-Malo, Brest, Saint-Nazaire, Nantes, La Pallice, the Gironde River, Saint-Jean-de-Luz and the Channel Islands. Over 30,000 troops were evacuated from Cherbourg alone; the final troopship left with German troops only 3 miles from the harbour. Lieutenant General James Marshall-Cornwall, in charge of the Cherbourg evacuation, recorded, 'All weapons were removed, except one 3.7inch A.A. gun, which broke down and was rendered unserviceable, and one static Bofors gun which could not be removed in time. Two anti-tank guns also had to be abandoned during the withdrawal.' From the other side, Tschimpke wrote: 'Thousands of lorries, cars and motorcycles are lined up and lined up on the UK's miles of dockside docks. Innumerable pieces of all possible war equipment lie between them. Nothing is more evidence of the hasty flight of the remains of the English troops than this confused jumble of pieces of uniform, weapons, and crates of food.'

Digue de Querqueville (Querqueville breakwater) with Fort de Chavagnac in the background. The French Navy anti-aircraft gun is a 37mm Mle 33. Its strategic value obvious, Cherbourg was heavily fortified by Napoleon in the nineteenth century. Another period of construction followed the 1898 'Fashoda Incident' – a series of imperial territorial disputes between Britain and France – with modernisation of seaward-facing forts and a new series of forts constructed on the landward side. After falling into German hands in June 1940, Allied planners recognised the capture of the port as a vital prerequisite in any future invasion of France and it would become one of the most important objectives of the D-Day landings on 6 June 1944. Heavily fortified as part of Germany's *Atlantikwall*, Hitler ordered Festung (fortress) Cherbourg to be held to the last man. It fell on 12 September 1944.

Le monument à Napoléon was erected in 1858 during a visit by Napoleon III to commemorate the establishment of the military port of Cherbourg by Napoleon I. The 5-metre-high bronze statue depicts Napoleon I on his Arabian horse, Marengo, which he rode during the Battle of Waterloo. Restoration work carried out in 2015 included the filling of forty-two bullet impacts received during the Second World War.

Cherbourg, with the Arsenal de la Marine in the background. The crane and seaplane hangars are part of the Base d'hydravions de la Marine de Cherbourg-Chantereyne. Smoke rises on the rear right from the Îlot de la Majorité along Quai Duperré from an earlier artillery and dive-bombing attack. Admiral Jean-Marie Charles Abrial had relocated his command post to Cherbourg after the evacuation of Dunkirk. Like the majority of similar ports, most of the smaller guns had been transferred to Paris or to the banks of the Seine River for anti-tank defence. Apart from a few second-rate battalions, the main defenders of the port were non-combat personnel such as mechanics, yeomen and air technicians. French resistance, however, enabled the evacuation of British troops and all French naval ships in the harbour. Dockyard workers sabotaged the submarines *Roland Morillot* and *La Praya*, then under construction, as well as ships moored in the harbour. Coastal batteries and forts along the main breakwater were also destroyed.

German troops in the centre of Querqueville.

Looking east from from the bridge leading to Querqueville Fort at the moat and escarpment wall.

Looking west from from the bridge leading to Querqueville Fort towards one of the hangars at the Querqueville naval air base (*Base d'aéronautique navale* – BAN). Behind the hangar stands a water tower with a windsock on top. This reinforced concrete hangar was built in 1925 by Ets. R. Sottile and the Bétons Armés Hennebique companies. It was followed by a second steel hangar, built in 1936 by Delattre et Frouard. The airfield was decommissioned in June 1969 to make way for a naval training centre. The hangars were demolished in the mid-1980s.

The interior of the steel hangar at the Querqueville naval air base. The aircraft in the centre of the photo is a Caudron C.445 Goeland. To the left is a Morane-Saulnier M.S.406 fighter. Units still present on the morning of 18 June 1940 included the Escadrille *A.B.1* (1st bomber squadron), part of the Flottille *F.1C.* (1st Fighter Flotilla) and the Groupe de Chasse G.C. 2/8 (French Air Force Fighter Group 2/8).

Inside one of the two Dubois-Lepeu hangars, built in the 1920s in the southern end of the Cherbourg-Chantereyne airbase. The structures visible in the background are radio masts. Units still present at Chantereyne naval air base (used exclusively by seaplanes) on the morning of 18 June 1940 were the 1.S1 squadron (action and surveillance squadron of the 1st Naval Region) and the T2 torpedo squadron.

Rommel met with French naval representatives gathered on the roof of the artillery command post at the Redoute des Couplets during the afternoon of 19 June, to discuss the surrender of Cherbourg.

Rommel in discussion with Capitaine de Corvette Henri Millière following an earlier ultimatum for an unconditional surrender by 1.15 p.m. French casualties during the German artillery and Ju 87 Stuka bombardment of the French maritime forts compelled Vice Admiral Jules Le Bigot to notify Admiral Jean-Marie Charles Abrial that the situation was untenable. He called for the fighting to stop. Millière then left by car from the Préfecture Maritime (naval headquarters) to negotiate with Rommel. At the same time, Capitaine de Corvette (R) Jean Boisserie arrived from Fort Querqueville. At Millière's request, Rommel dictated his terms of surrender – an immediate ceasefire with white flags flown above each fort; NCOs were to take charge of the men and march along the road to Les Pieux carrying their personal kit and essential rations; officers were to assemble in the Préfecture Maritime with their batmen and all weapons were to be unloaded and stacked within the forts. After German troops entered Cherbourg at 3.30 p.m., a formal surrender would be held in the Préfecture Maritime.

French naval officers at Redoute des Couplets during the German bombardment negotiate the surrender of Cherbourg. The French naval officer, 'with a long black beard', is Capitaine de Corvette (R) Jean Boisserie (1896–1963). To his right is Millière (1896–1976). Apparently horrified by his fort cloaked in smoke by the bombardment, Boisserie asked the German general why it was being attacked when it had already ceased fire. 'Because it has not surrendered,' Rommel replied.

The anchor on both sides of the helmeted French sailor's overcoat collar denotes non-petty officer personnel (Équipages de la Flotte). Boisserie (wearing a peaked cap) and Millière (wearing a 1939 model helmet) have jackets with four stripes sewn on the lower sleeve, signifying their rank as Capitaine de Corvette.

Major Eduard Crasemann (on Rommel's right) was commander of the II Battalion of the 78th Artillery Regiment. In May 1941, Crasemann joined Rommel in North Africa as commander of the 33rd Motorised Artillery Regiment and later the 15th Panzer Division. Crasemann returned to Europe in January 1943. He served on the Eastern Front and Italy before commanding the XII SS Corps in the defence of the Rhineland. In 1947, he was tried by a British War Crimes Tribunal for involvement in the mass execution of 175 Italian civilians (including twenty-six children and sixty-three women) by the 26th Panzer Division in Padule di Fucecchio, Tuscany, in August 1944. He died in prison on 28 April 1950, aged 59.

The series of photographs at Redoute des Couplets was taken on the roof of the *poste de commandement d'artillerie* (artillery command post).

Cherbourg was declared an 'open city' on 19 June. Seated with a map of Cherbourg, Rommel negotiates a surrender with Léon Vaur (1895–1994), popular Democrat MP for the Cherbourg constituency. He is one of the two leading figures from the town of Cherbourg who met Rommel at Équeurdreville on the morning of 19 June. This meeting, at 'a point half a mile north of the Redoute des Couplets', according to Rommel's *Papers*, took place at the 'Villa Ane', where this photograph was probably taken. Rommel recalled the meeting: 'I had just sent a radio message to Major Heidkämper informing him of the progress of the attack, when Oberst [Friedrich] Fürst arrived from the eastern side of Querqueville with the news that Oberst von Bismarck was in negotiation there with a deputation from the town. This was probably a direct result of the division's leaflets calling on the garrison to surrender.'

Rommel and staff outside the Villa Ane, still standing, at the intersection of Rue des Goths (nowadays Rue Ango), Rue de la Paix and Chasse de la Saline (nowadays Rue de la Saline). Oberst Georg von Bismarck, 7th Rifle Brigade, had earlier met with Mr Léon Vaur and Commissaire Laniez, deputy special commissioner, at the site, the brigade's forward headquarters.

Photograph taken from Villa Ane towards a group of houses located along the Chasse de la Saline, with the Cherbourg arsenal burning in the background.

Opposite: 19 June 1940. Rommel and officers of the 7th Panzer-Division assemble in the Préfecture Maritime, opposite a French delegation to receive Cherbourg's surrender at 5 p.m. French delegates had already assured Rommel of their agreement with the terms of surrender and a ceasefire was called. Surrender conditions were radioed to the various forts in the city. Rich in National Socialist overtones, Alfred Tschimpke's 1940 account reads: 'The German general [Rommel] is standing in the garden of the naval headquarters in the middle of the city. In front of him the commanders of his regiments and detachments. A colonel reports. With terse words, his hand on his cap, the general thanks the troops for their service as a soldier. "The pace was fast. The utmost was demanded of man and material, but it should be. Success has justified these efforts. Thank you!" On the other side of the garden, the French officers listened in silence to the brief speech. Next to the general is an interpreter, a French sailor with the characteristic tuft of red wool on his cap. "I have taken note of the surrender of the city and fortress of Cherbourg. You have avoided unnecessary bloodshed in the last hour!" The general has spoken. The five French admirals, including the commander of the sea fortress, with the officers of their staffs, put their hands on their caps. At this moment the English admiral [Vice Admiral Bertram Ramsay] descends the stairs of the command building. The same one who had opposed the surrender. He is late. You don't pay attention to him. … Brief negotiations with the mayor of the city follow. Everything is done in five minutes.'

The French delegation assembled at Cherbourg's Préfecture Maritime. Left to right: Général de Brigade Marie Goudouneix (wearing the helmet) was the Général adjoint au Préfet Maritime (General assistant to the Maritime Prefect) to Vice Admiral Le Bigot; Vice-Amiral d'Escadre Jules Le Bigot, wearing a peaked cap and jacket with four stars on the lower sleeve, was Commandant en chef, Préfet Maritime de la 1ère Région Maritime, Gouverneur de la place (Commander in chief, Maritime Prefect of 1st Naval Region and Governor of the place); Contre-Amiral (Rear Admiral) Jean Le Bonzec, on the right, wearing a peaked cap with two stars on his lower jacket sleeve, was the *major* général commanding the Cherbourg naval dockyard and arsenal. Unseen are the legion of German filmmakers and photographers who have followed the 7th Panzer Division through France.

Sullen-faced officers, left to right: Général de Brigade Marie Goudouneix; the naval officer with peaked cap with five stripes (three gold and two silver) could be Capitaine de Frégate (Commander) Émile Tranier, Chief of Communication of 1ère Région Maritime (1st Naval Region); Vice-Amiral d'Escadre Jules Le Bigot and Contre-Amiral Jean Le Bonzec.

French naval and army officers watch the surrender proceedings from the opposite side of the Préfecture Maritime courtyard. After covering a distance of 220 miles (354km) over four days to reach Cherbourg, Rommel dashed off a letter to Lu explaining, 'There had been bad moments for us and the enemy was at first between twenty and forty times our number.' Nevertheless, he had succeeded in accomplishing Hitler's 'special order' to seize Cherbourg as quickly as possible.

Under Rommel's watchful eye, Amiral Jean Abrial (left), wearing a peaked cap and five stars on his jacket sleeve, receives a translation of the surrender terms from a French seaman. Abrial, who was Amiral Nord, the commander of French naval forces for Northern France (Channel), had withdrawn from Dunkirk to Cherbourg on 10 June 1940 and established a new headquarters at Château de Tourlaville, 1.2 miles (2km) east of Cherbourg. According to Rommel's account, Abrial was originally not present at the Préfecture Maritime and had to be escorted there by the divisional liaison officer, Captain Christoph von Platen. Standing behind Abrial is his *chef d'état-major* (chief of staff), Contre-Amiral Marcel Leclerc. Rommel began the ceremony by thanking his officers for their role in the capture of Cherbourg. After acknowledging Vice-Amiral d'Escadre Le Bigot through a French interpreter for stopping useless bloodshed, Le Bigot replied that he 'would not have surrendered if I still had ammunition and armaments'. A similar overture prompted Abrial to add: 'The surrender of Cherbourg is a fact, but I have nothing to do with it.' Resolute in sharing the same fate as his men, Abrial forewent an opportunity to escape with Le Bigot. His orderly recounted how he raised the idea of evading capture and donning civilian clothes. '*Mon pauvre ami* [my poor friend], there is no escape for us. We have given our word.' From the victors' perspective, von Luck observed that Rommel was 'very courteous' during the ceremony and paid tribute to the French garrison. His fair attitude, which he showed towards the defeated garrison, 'earned him respect – even abroad'.

Cherbourg surrenders. Left to right: A French naval officer, the three stripes on his sleeve denoting a *lieutenant de vaisseau* (lieutenant); Amiral Jean Abrial; and a French seaman relaying Rommel's terms.

The French sailor (possibly an interpreter) on the left was seen earlier with Capitaine de Corvette Henri Millière at the Redoute des Couplets. The French officer beside him could be Capitaine de Vaisseau Raoul Pérot, the *arrondissement*, chief of staff of 1ère Région Maritime (1st Naval Region).

Left to right: Vice-Amiral d'Escadre Jules Le Bigot, Contre-Amiral Jean Le Bonzec, the French translator, and Rommel.

Centre to right: Vice-Amiral d'Escadre Jules Le Bigot, Contre-Amiral Jean Le Bonzec, a *capitaine de frégate* (see above) and Contre-Amiral Jean Le Bonzec.

Victor and vanquished pictured after formalities concluded. The senior French naval officers were subsequently imprisoned for a year in Königstein castle, 25 miles (40km) from Dresden, in the German province of Saxony. Later, at Admiral François Darlan's request, the captive French naval officers were released to oversee the French Navy under the Vichy government.

Rommel pictured with Major i.G. Otto Heidkämper. Only a week earlier, on 13 June, Heidkämper had submitted a damming memorandum to Rommel outlining the difficulties his staff had with the general's methods. Rommel, in turn, castigated his subordinate officer in a letter home, complaining that he remained some 20 miles behind the front lines, fearful that something might happen to himself and divisional staff while losing contact with the *Kampfgruppe* (battle group) that Rommel was leading at Cambrai. The 'affair' was resolved after a couple of days – 'I went and saw Hoth and we had a long talk about the whole thing. I'm glad there's peace in the camp again.'

Swastika over Cherbourg. Together with Heidkämper, Rommel visited the Fort de Roule, with its commanding view over the town and harbour. In a etter home to Lu, he wrote that he had just slept for seven hours and was about to review his troops, the 'immense booty' accompanying his conquest and the 20,000 to 30,000 prisoners taken in and around Cherbourg. Tschimpke effused over the feat: 'The German general drives through the city. Many houses and streets show the traces of German artillery fire. The cars wind their way up the steep serpentine street to the central fort. At this moment, the swastika flag rises on the highest bastion. Bright red, it flutters in the sea breeze. The German division commander stands at the concrete parapet and looks down on the elongated cityscape of Cherbourg. Beside him are his regimental commanders. Below, out of the harbour, out of the numerous wharves, thick black smoke swells up. The broken concrete blocks of the forts show the terrible effect of the German Stuka attacks. On the parapets stand the German officers and soldiers. The uniforms are barely recognizable from dirt. Boots and skirts are torn. Smoke has blackened their faces. But their eyes are bright.'

Rommel crowed about the campaign to his wife, writing on 21 June 1940 that it had 'now gradually turned into a lightning tour of France'. The French armistice was signed the following day, near Compiègne.

In six weeks of fighting, Rommel had captured 97,648 prisoners – including 5 admirals, 1 corps commander and 4 divisional commanders and staff – and taken 458 armoured vehicles, 277 artillery pieces, 64 anti-tank guns, 458 tanks and armoured cars, over 4,000 trucks, over 1,500 cars and more than 1,550 horse-drawn vehicles. In the same period, the 7th Panzer Division suffered 682 men killed (including 52 officers), 1,646 wounded and 296 missing. Forty-two of its tanks were destroyed. In Hans von Luck's opinion, it was 'certainly a proud balance'. The 7th Panzer Division recorded how young German soldiers were astonished by the weak resistance offered by the French.

> After all, they had been told that the French were going to be tough foes. But even more astonished were the veterans of World War I; after all, they had gotten to know the *Poilu* [literally 'hairy one' – an informal term for the French infantryman dating back to Napoleonic times] during the battles around Verdun, along the Somme, in the Argonne and elsewhere as a brave fighter.

Hitler (standing centre with hand on hip) looks towards the statue of Ferdinand Foch, Supreme Allied Commander during the First World War, before starting armistice negotiations in the same railway car at Compiègne where the Armistice of 11 November 1918 was signed. With the signing of the French Franco–German armistice on 22 June 1940, the Frech Third Republic was dissolved. Germany would occupy the northern and western coasts of France, the so-called *zone occupé*. The remaining unoccupied south-eastern region, the *zone libre*, was overseen by 84-year-old Marshal Philippe Pétain's collaborationist Vichy government.

Whereas Hitler had anticpated more than a million casualties to conquer France, his six-week 'lightning' campiagn had cost Germany 27,074 killed, 111,034 wounded and 18,384 missing. French losses were 85,310 killed, 120,000 wounded, 12,000 missing and another 1.54 million taken prisoner. The BEF had lost some 10,000 killed and 68,000 casualties. Though outnumbered in arms and manpower, Germany overan France as a consequence of three primary factors: poor intelligence, plus tactical and operational shortcomings in conjunction with inadequate strategic leadership.

Chapter Five

Bordeaux Victory Parade

Fresh from a string of conquests, the 7th Panzer Division arrived in the port city of Bordeaux on 24 June 1940. 'At last the armistice is in force,' Rommel penned in a letter to his wife. 'We're now less than 200 miles from the Spanish frontier. … How wonderful it's all been.'

Earlier in the month, when Paris was threatened by the German advance, the French government had relocated to Bordeaux. Premier Paul Reynaud led a minority government, supported by Charles de Gaulle and Georges Mandel, which favoured a 'war to the finish'. Appeals for immediate assistance were sent to the United States and Britain, before Reynaud was overridden by the opposition. He resigned on 16 June – two days after German forces entered Paris. Bordeaux was later reoccupied by French forces, in August 1944.

Civilians pictured outside the fifteenth-century cathedral Saint-André de Bordeaux; German military vehicles are parked outside. This tower is crowned by a statue of Notre-Dame d'Aquitaine.

After Cherbourg surrendered, the 7th Panzer Division was sent south to Saintes on the Atlantic coast. It passed through the historic port and walled city of Saint-Malo on 21 June 1940. This is Rue Broussais, with Rue de La Harpe leading off to the left behind the Peugeot type 402. Also on the left is the *Librairie-Papeterie Maritime* bookshop; on the right is the *Patisserie Armange*. In the distance, a sign above the Sd.Kfz. 263 (8-Rad) advertises the *Pharmacie du Marché* on Place du Marché aux legumes. The tables would turn on 17 August 1944, when Germans defenders under Oberst Andreas von Aulock in Festung Saint-Malo (Fortress Saint-Malo) surrendered to the US 83rd Infantry Division after two weeks of heavy fighting. Concentrated bombing and shelling had left only 182 out of 865 buildings still standing.

A Brückengerät spans the Loire River at Ancenis. Pictured behind Rommel, on the northern bank of the river, is a captured Humber Pullman limousine (with swastika on the hood) and an Opel Kapitän.

French engineers blew up the former suspension bridge at Ancenis (inaugurated on 1 May 1839) on 19 June 1940, to stop the German advance at the Loire. It was temporarily rebuilt, and destroyed again in 1944. These two photos were likely taken when Rommel and his division crossed the Loire River en route to Bordeaux, some 220 miles (354km) to south.

Bordeaux and the Garonne River. German columns taking part in a victory parade on 1 July 1940 crossed the river from Pont de Pierre.

Victory Parade

Rommel, in the presence of General der Infanterie Hermann Hoth, at the divisional victory parade. The saluting base is situated on Quai Louis XVII facing the Place des Quinconces. The parade order was (see Appenidix 1):

1) Panzer-Aufklärungs-Abteilung 37
2) Kradschützen-Bataillon 7
3) Schützen-Regiment 6 and 3. Kompanie/Fla-Bataillon 59
4) Panzer-Nachrichten-Abteilung 83
5) Artillerie-Regiment 78 and II. Abteilung/Artillerie-Regiment 45
6) Panzerjäger-Abteilung 42
7) Panzer-Pionier-Bataillon 58
8) Schützen-Regiment 7
9) Pionier-Bataillon 627 (motorisiert)
10) Korps-Nachrichten-Abteilung 61 [XV. Armeekorps (motorisiert)].

Hoth reviews Rommel's so-called 'Ghost Division'. Success in the French campaign led to Hoth's promotion to Generaloberst on 19 July 1940, during a victory speech by Hitler in Berlin.

A beaming Generalmajor Erwin Rommel, wearing a parade helmet.

Looking south along the Quai Louis XVIII. The car is a mittlerer Einheits-PKW Kfz. 15; the armoured car in the distance is a Sd.Kfz. 231 Sechs-Rad. Note the pennants on the lamppost: the lower one is the division with the tactical marking of the 7th Panzer Division in yellow; the upper one is the marking of a Korps/Korpskommando or Kommandierender General.

BMW 326 cabriolet staff car.

Parading motorcyclists from either Kraftradschützenbataillon 7 (7th Motorcycle Battalion) or the Kradschützenkompanie of the Panzeraufklärungsabteilung 37 (37th Panzer Reconnaissance Battalion).

Two leichte Panzerspähwagen (Fu) Sd.Kfz. 223 light armoured radio cars lead two Panzerfunkwagen Sd.Kfz. 263 (8-Rad) armoured radio vehicles.

A schwerer Panzerspähwagen Sd.Kfz. 231 (6-Rad) precedes a pair of Sd.Kfz. 222 armoured cars.

Rommel rides in an Opel 'Admiral' Cabriolet, flying the divisional pennant. A mittlerer Einheits-PKW Kfz. 15 is parked on the other side of the street, near the beginning of the Place des Quinconces.

Eyes right. Two mittlerer Zugkraftwagen 5t (Sd.Kfz. 6) half-tracks haul 10.5cm le. FH 18 light howitzers. This medium 5-ton vehicle was primarily used to tow these guns as well as the 10cm s. K. 18 and heavier 15cm s. FH 18 guns.

The leichte Zugkraftwagen 1t (Sd.Kfz. 10) was a light 1-ton half-track designed to tow light loads such as a 3.7cm Pak.

A Sd.Kfz. 251 Ausf. A half-track tows a 10.5cm le. FH 18 light howitzer.

Krupp L2H143 (popularly known as the Krupp Protze), a 6x4 truck towing a 7.5cm le IG (with solid metal wheels and rubber tyres for motorised transport) passes before the XV Armeekorps band.

Booty. A captured British Bedford MWD truck, 15cwt, 4x2 towing 3.7cm Pak 36.

Looking to the north along Quai Louis XVIII. Left to right: Ford type V 8-51, second Krupp L 2 H 143 MTW (Mannschaftstransportwagen), Ford type V 8-51.

A post-war postcard of Quai Louis XVIII. Hoth and Rommel reviewed the parade between the poles visible in the foreground (right).

Rommel's achievements in France stirred up jealously among many fellow officers. Others held reservations. Hermann Hoth wrote a confidential report that recommended a corps command for Rommel only after additional experience and an improved sense of judgement. He criticised the commander of the 'Ghost Division' for his tendency to act impulsively. In public, a different side was presented. Hoth applauded his success at a divisional dinner, 'under the influence of much alcohol', lambasting his predecessor, General Georg Stumme, as a 'lame old carthorse' in comparison to the more dynamic Rommel.

Geheime Kommandosache!

Der Oberbefehlshaber
der 4. Armee
Ia Nr. 741/40 g.Kdos.

A. H. Qu., den 30. Nov. 1940.

Dem Kommandeur der 7. Panzer-Division,
Herrn Generalmajor Rommel.

Mein lieber Rommel !

Für die Übersendung der Geschichte der 7.Panzer-Division in den Monaten Mai und Juni 1940 danke ich Ihnen aufrichtig. Ich habe die Darstellung mit hohem Interesse gelesen und in der anschaulichen Schilderung meine bisherige Auffassung, dass hier überragenden Leistungen vorliegen, voll bestätigt gefunden.

Aus Ihrer Bitte um ein Vorwort schliesse ich, dass Sie eine Veröffentlichung dieser Divisionsgeschichte beabsichtigen. Ich muss Sie jedoch darauf aufmerksam machen, dass eine solche nach den zur Zeit gültigen Zensurbestimmungen nicht zulässig ist, weil die Schilderung weit über den Rahmen der Führerrede und der Wehrmachtsberichte Einzelheiten bringt. Fremde militärische Dienststellen könnten durch sie Einblick in unsere Führungsgrundsätze gewinnen, noch dazu in unsere Art der Verwendung grosser Panzerverbände, was nach dem eindeutig ausgesprochenen Willen des Führers unbedingt verhindert werden muss. Diese Geheimhaltung scheint mir auch bei Ausgabe an einen begrenzten Kreis nicht voll gesichert, und ich bitte Sie daher, vor einer Veröffentlichung oder der Ausgabe an untere Dienststellen die Genehmigung Ihrer vorgesetzten Stellen bis zum O.K.H. einschliesslich einzuholen. Für eine Veröffentlichung ist auch das Einverständnis des O.K.W./W Pr. nötig.

Für den Fall dieser Genehmigung und unter der Voraussetzung, dass einige von mir nachstehend auseinandergesetzte Änderungswünsche berücksichtigt werden, stelle ich Ihnen das beiliegende Vorwort zur Verfügung.

Mit diesem Vorwort sanktioniere ich gewissermassen die Gesamtdarstellung und damit auch einige Sätze, derentwegen ich Bedenken habe. Ich bin gewiss, dass die gegenwärtige Fassung der Darstellung sich aus Ihren Unterlagen einwandfrei ergibt. Jedoch entspringt sie dann dem Blickfeld der Division und fügt sich nicht ganz in das Bild der grossen Operation ein. Auch könnten ausserhalb der Division stehende Persönlichkeiten sich durch sie verletzt fühlen, was Sie bestimmt ebensowenig beabsichtigen wie ich. Um jeder Mißstimmung zuvorzukommen, bitte ich Sie daher um einige Änderungen.

- 2 -

Günther von Kluge thanked Rommel for his manuscript, which he read with 'great interest', before stressing how the content of such a book could provide foreign agencies with an insight into the Wehrmacht's leadership and use of armoured formations. Moreover, Rommel's view of the fighting was questioned, with changes requested, for example, about the fighting on 21 May and unwarranted criticism of the 5th Panzer Division on 22 May and during the capture of the bridge at Landrecies. The involvement of the Luftwaffe was mentioned only twice – once on 15 May, during the attack on Philippeville, and later on 5 June, during the fighting at Hangest.

Rommel authored an 'enhanced' history of the 7th Panzer Division after the French campaign, a sequel to his earlier *Infanterie Greift an*. It met with immediate resistance. Günther von Kluge, whom Rommel invited to write a foreword to the manuscript, pointed out that several diagrams and references overstated the division's record. The vital part played by the Luftwaffe, especially by Ju 87 dive-bombers, was all but ignored. The advance of the 32nd Infantry Division was portrayed as slower than it actually was. Disparaging references were also given to the neighbouring 5th Panzer Division after the commanding officer, General Max von Hartlieb-Walsporn, had formally criticised Rommel. General Franz Halder refused to send Rommel the official photographs he requested for the preparation of an illustrated book while General Johannes Streich (whom Rommel would later dismiss for poor performance at Tobruk) was critical of Rommel's losses: 'The '7th Panzer Division took far heavier casualties [for example, 682 men killed compared to 267 deaths in the 1st Panzer Division] than any other division in the west, including infantry divisions.' In another controversial act, Rommel recommended Karl Hanke for the Knight's Cross until the latter offended Rommel by mentioning to a Propaganda Ministry secretary that *his* rank outweighed Rommel as a major general. Furious, Rommel dispatched an adjutant to intercept the bravery citation before it reached Berlin, an action, according to a tank commander, that 'became common knowledge' within the division and 'badly tarnished the image that all of his troops had gained of him on account of his courage and genius as leader'.

Nazi propaganda naturally extolled Rommel's decisive part in the conquest of France, 'like one of the Horsemen of the Apocalypse'. Glorified in the press, radio and publications like Tschimpke's *Die Gespenster-Division*, Rommel's name became synonymous with blitzkrieg. The word '*Rommeln*' was even coined to label a rapid, bold advance, as portrayed in the feature-length propaganda film *Sieg im Westen* (*Victory in the West*). Fashioning a hero, one propagandist wrote: 'yes, they know him now in France – they know this face, with its blue eyes and their hint of hidden cunning.' Lauding his triumph, Tschimpke described the general late in the campaign:

> sitting on the ground, his back against a tree trunk, his eyes half closed. And in his mind those three weeks and the many miles of foreign space that he has traversed … Tanks demystified the extended Maginot Line's reputation for supposed invincibility. The Somme has lost its horror.

Meanwhile in Berlin, General Franz Halder turned to his diary, noting:

> the near future will show whether Britain will do the reasonable thing in the light of our victories or will try to carry on the war singlehanded. In the latter case, the war will lead to Britain's destruction and may last a long time.

Returning to the coast after participating in the filming of *Sieg im Westen*, Rommel's division prepared for Hitler's (aborted) seaborne invasion of England by practising for an amphibious landing from river barges improvised as landing craft. Promoted to the rank of Generalleutnant in January 1941, Rommel was dispatched to Libya to lead *Unternehmen*

Sonnenblume (Operation Sunflower) in early February in the wake of Britain's hugely successful offensive against the Italians. It was in North Africa that he would earn the reputation of the 'Desert Fox' and receive his marshal's baton.

Preis: 20 Pfennig
Frankreich 4 frs.

DONNERSTAG, 8. OKTOBER 1942
17. JAHRGANG . • . FOLGE 41

JB Illustrierter Beobachter

Mit herzlichen Heimatgrüßen an die Front von:

VERLAG FRANZ EHER NACHF. GmbH MÜNCHEN 22

Copyright 1942 by Franz Eher Nachf., G. m. b. H., München 22

Generalfeldmarschall Rommel beim Führer.

Der Führer empfing am 30. September den Oberbefehlshaber der Panzerarmee Afrikas, Generalfeldmarschall Rommel, zum Vortrag. Der Führer überreichte bei dieser Gelegenheit Marschall Rommel den Marschallstab und sprach dem verdienten Armeeführer nochmals zugleich im Namen des deutschen Volkes seinen Dank und seine Anerkennung aus.

Aufnahme: Heinrich Hoffmann.

Generalfeldmarschall Rommel is presented with his marshal's baton by Hitler on 30 September 1942, while in Europe for medical treatment, his Panzerarmee checked at El Alamein.

Part II

Chapter Six

Re-enacting the Somme Crossing

War moves across the fields
Up and down the streets
Many a soldier's grave
Lies in the dim woods

Song from the German propaganda film
Sieg im Westen

In August 1940, Rommel was invited to re-enact his role in the fighting and provide additional footage for a new propaganda film. More than eighty years after the event, manufactured scenes from this propaganda film are still commonly used to portray the fighting in June 1940, the 'Blitzkrieg in the West'.

The Second World War was also a cleverly fought propaganda war. Reichspropagandaminister Joseph Goebbels was delighted by the 'splendid success' of the documentary film *Feldzug in Polen* (*Campaign in Poland*), which premiered in Berlin on 8 February 1940. Having 'hit the bulls', as he termed it, the German populace flocked to watch the story of Nazi Germany's first campaign. Reaction to the film was overwhelmingly positive, with reviewers lauding the film's apparent realism. As a writer for the Nazi Party's *Völkischer Beobachter* opined, there was no need for well-known actors, producers or writers since

Film posters and programme. 'Propaganda, propaganda, propaganda,' Adolf Hitler said after the failed 1923 Munich putsch. 'All that matters is propaganda.'

history had delivered the script, the German soldier fulfilling the role of main actor. A second film on the campaign, *Feuertaufe* (*Baptism of Fire*) followed. Hitler's 1940 offensive was the subject of the 1941 feature-length film *Sieg im Westen* (*Victory in the West*). Produced from nearly a million feet of carefully edited newsreel footage taken during and after the fighting, it was directed by Svend Noldan and Fritz Brunel, with a running time of 114 minutes. The film was produced by the Oberkommando des Heeres and featured a clear narrative beginning with the Thirty Years War (1618–48), followed by the history of the German nation including the humiliation suffered under the Treaty of Versailles after the First World War. A voice-over explained the film as the 'fight of the German people that has been called many times over the centuries to defend its borders and its living space [*Lebensraum*]'. Scenes of peace within Germany preceded footage showing the invasion of the Low Countries and France under Hitler's 'infallible' leadership. Rommel was asked to participate, both in front of and behind the camera, to recreate the crossing of the Somme in August 1940, a role for which he was later uncredited. The film premiered on 31 January 1941.

Hans Ertl, seen here in North Africa, was responsible for the filming of the re-enacted scenes of Rommel crossing the Somme. Ertl, a well-known *Die Deutsch Wochenschau* newsreel cameraman, had earlier photographed the Olympic Games in Berlin in 1936 and worked for famous Nazi-era filmmaker Leni Riefenstahl. Ertl received orders to shoot additional scenes of the fighting at the Somme because the available rushes were considered unsuitable. Filming was carried out under his direction in collaboration with Rommel and Karl Rothenburg. Ertl wrote that Rommel received him 'like an old acquaintance because of my brief debut in his command vehicle, some three months earlier in battle at Cassel-Poperinghe' (in Belgium). The general 'rubbed his chin with a smile as he looked over the proposed list of film shoots and noted how the agenda was almost a repeat of his earlier tank raids. In just one hour we agreed on a few effective scenes that were to be undertaken over several days during autumn manoeuvres.' The two men would meet again in North Africa, where Ertl became known as 'Rommel's photographer'. Banned from working professionally in Germany after the war, Ertl moved to Bolivia in 1950. He published his memoirs in 1985 and died in 2000, aged 92.

German vehicles cross the Somme Canal at Condé-Folie (midway between Amiens and Abbeville) under simulated enemy attack. The railway and road bridges were left intact by the French, who intended to counterattack north of the Somme. German engineers unbolted rails and removed sleepers to allow divisional vehicles to use the lower bridge. Rommel wrote in his *Papers* that he left his vehicle on the north side of the Somme, giving instructions to the crew to be the first vehicle to cross. He then walked across the bridges with Leutnant Luft and signals staff. Rommel's signals vehicle crossed the river at 0600 hours, followed by artillery, anti-aircraft units and the tanks of the 25th Panzer Regiment.

Another aerial photo taken from a Henschel 126 reveals the two intact rail bridges. At least three light aircraft participated in the filming: two Hs-126 and one Fieseler Storch (Fi-156). Tschimpke's *Die Gespenster-Division* recounted the horror associated with the bloody First World War Somme battles. 'Anyone who had been to Verdun or fought in the summer battles knew the war in its most devastating form. … The dirty black river that runs through the green hills below the high bank slopes. It looks so harmless, no more threatening than other rivers. And yet tens of thousands made their way through hell, a quarter of a century ago, jumping from trench to trench, competing with death, which had threatened millions of times. They lay in the fire, days, weeks, months. And for what? A few miserable kilometers of this battered land were all they gained.' Tschimpke could gloat, 'The Somme has lost its terror. And three days later it will be the Seine. The Seine, that's Paris. Paris is France.'

A report from an infantry regiment that made the original assault across the Somme in June 1940 at Condé-Folie noted:

> The locality [proved] a particularly difficult point to reduce. Our troops again met stiff resistance, the enemy fighting with ferocity. The Blacks in particular utilised every opportunity to stage a defence to the bitter end. … Many comrades-in-arms met their deaths there, but we had to take the place. … These were difficult hours: the enemy defended every house, and every window and skylight was spitting fire at us. To break this resistance, once-and-for-all, we then brought flame-throwers into action before our fusiliers bravely plunged with grenades and bayonets into hand-to-hand combat, thus to subdue this important position.

A camera on the riverbank captures the action from a different vantage point.

A Hs 126 short-range reconnaissance and army cooperation aircraft pictured from a Fieseler Storch also participating in the filming.

A Pz.Kpfw. IV pair and infantry cross one of the bridges over the Somme Canal.

An image originally captioned *Die letzte Brűcke* ('The last bridge') in the *Sieg im Westen* movie. 'Through a bold stroke this bridge over the Somme had been saved from the enemy. Our armour crossed it under enemy artillery attack that pushed water as high as a fountain while smoke like fog enveloped the passage of vehicles. The enemy was no longer able to destroy the bridge.'

German infantry 'seize' a bridge while an NCO, without helmet, casually leans against the wall, looking on.

Filming continues with a tripod-mounted 35mm cine camera mounted on the roof of a Mercedes-Benz type 230 Pullman-Limousine. Note the dismantled rail sleepers and rails pushed to the side of the embankment.

Having crossed the Somme Canal (top left corner), the German armour was brought to a stop when Pz.Kpfw. IV '321' lost its right track on the approach to a road bridge. The former rail line at this point ran from Flixecourt to Hangest-sur-Somme.

Pz.Kpfw. IV '321' would later 'star' in the recreated capture of Château le Quesnoy, some 5 miles distant. Note the absence of helmets and the 'spectators' in this non-combat setting.

Rommel oversees efforts to right the precariously situated Pz.Kpfw. IV '321' using tow cables attached to the Pz.Kpfw. 38(t).

Another view of disabled Pz.Kpfw. IV '321'. Note Hans Ertl, standing with handheld cine camera on the embankment beside the bridge. (*Personal collection of Dr Thierry Moné – reproduced with kind permission*)

A cable is attached to '321' to help guide it down the slope.

In his *Papers*, Rommel narrates the scene quite differently: 'A Panzer IV had shed its right track and was blocking the entire passage. … Attempts were being made to drag the tank bodily forwards, with little success as the sleepers were jamming in the rubber rollers and pushing the ballast along in front of them. A good half-hour was lost while the Panzer IV was pulled and pushed across the bridge, by other tanks.'

Pz.Kpfw. IV '321' and the camera car are now at the bottom of the embankment while traffic flows freely across the bridge. Two Sd.Kfz. 251 half-tracks towing artillery have crossed the bridge, a captured British Austin Type K2 truck follows.

After crossing the Somme, a Pz.Kpfw. 38(t) is pictured at speed along the road perpendicular to a valley in which the division would gather. *Propagandakompanie* (PK) photographer Eric Borchert's photo was captioned simply: 'On the road ahead.'

The schwerer geländegängiger Personenkraftwager (schwerer Einheits-PKW), literally translated as a 'heavy cross-country standard-passenger car', was built by both Horch and Ford Germany using their specific V-8 engine from 1937 to 1942. The Mannschaftskraftwagen (personnel carrier) *Kfz.* 70 had a crew of eight, including the driver.

Aerial views of the path taken by advancing German vehicles beside the railway line and then through the small valley.

A Pz.Kpfw. II and Pz.Kpfw. 38 (t) pass several stationary Opel Blitz S 3-ton trucks.

The Kfz. 69 Protzkraftwagen, the most common version of the Krupp L2 H 143, with a 3.7cm Pak and crew.

A Sd.Kfz. 251, its crew exposed, and 10.5cm le. FH 18 howitzer. Note the 'K' symbol, identifying the vehicle attached to Panzergruppe von Kleist.

Another aerial view of soft-skin and armoured vehicles massing in the valley.

'An endless column marches ....' After crossing the railway bridge, the procession of vehicles proceeds along the road before retracing their route into a valley. Combat distances were in the order of 20 metres between the vehicles travelling at 20km/h, 25 meters when 25km/h, 30 meters when 30km/h. But a dispersed formation in depth would have distances of 100 to 200 metres between vehicles.

Soft-skin vehicles and motorcyclists approach the valley (left); tank crews at rest (right).

Hans Ertl changes a cine camera film canister during the staged advance. (*Personal collection of Dr Thierry Moné – reproduced with kind permission*)

Hans Ertl recounted an 'unforgettable' first scene – 'a bird's eye view from a hill into a large grassy valley blanketed in a morning mist that was suddenly pulled away as if by the fist of an invisible giant, unveiling hundreds of tanks … the ominous drone of powerful engines rolled up to my camera position like a threatening storm.'

A parade-like mass of vehicles fills the valley. Many of the film's recreated scenes are still used in documentaries depicting the might of the Wehrmacht during the 1940 blitzkrieg. Notwithstanding the circumstances here, provisional guidelines issued in January 1941 for the deployment of tanks stipulated: 'One should always strive to have tracked and wheeled vehicles separated. This measure reduces strain on vehicles. … Vehicles that stay with tracked vehicles include command cars, communication, maintenance vehicles and ambulances as well as the most essential trucks with fuel and rations.'

Pz.Kpfw. IIs and Pz.Kpfw. 38(t)s beside the wreck of an Opel Blitz – a relic from the June fighting used as a prop in the filming. The narration in *Sieg im Westen* explains how this force is 'positioned, ready to attack', the German war machine seemingly invincible.

The same Opel Blitz, damaged during the actual fighting in June 1940 and pictured from the air before the August 'battle'. (*Personal collection of Dr Thierry Moné – reproduced with kind permission*)

No sign of combat readiness, as required when passing through hostile territory, in this low-level photograph snapped from a Fieseler Fi 156 Storch (Stork).

Hans von Luck recalled how Rommel, seen here with binoculars, 'was already somewhat vain, but we were happy to overlook this. He always had his camera on hand, to photograph the most important scenes.' During the campaign he wrote to his wife, requesting that she cut out all newspaper articles that featured him.

Rommel beside a Pz.Kpfw. IV with a Leica IIID camera, likely the one Reichspropagandaminister Goebbels presented to him before the 1940 Western Campaign.

Infantry from Schützen Regiment 6 scale the steep valley slope beside the railway line in a reconstructed 'attack' against French defenders above. They carry a Mauser Karabiner 98 Kurz (or K98), the Wehrmacht's standard bolt-action service rifle.

A heavy mortar crew assembles their 8cm Granatwerfer 34 (8cm GrW 34). Broken down into three parts – baseplate, bipod and smoothbore barrel – for transport, this was the German Army's standard *mittler* (medium) mortar during the war. A trained crew could fire from fifteen to twenty-five rounds in a minute.

The mortar projectile, stabilised in flight by small fins in the tail, was dropped down the smoothbore barrel where a firing pin in the base ignited a propellant charge. The projectile was thrust upwards on a trajectory determined by careful aiming of the weapon via separate traversing and aiming hand-wheels. The mortar fired conventional high explosive (HE) and smoke bombs plus the special 8cm Wurfgranate 39 ('bouncing bomb') that sprang upwards upon detonation of an initial charge to a height of approximately 5 to 10 feet before the main TNT charge was detonated, simulating an air-burst round.

A mix of armour emerges from the valley – the same moment caught from the air (above) and on the ground (below). Note the crewmember of the Pz.Kpfw. IV astride the 7.5cm cannon.

A miscellany of soft-skin vehicles. In the centre is a schwerer Einheits-PKW; the vehicle in the foreground is a mittlerer Einheits-PKW; facing the opposite direction is a Phänomen Granit 25H ambulance. The trucks parked on the far right are Mercedes-Benz, possibly type L 3000.

'The wide meadows were still covered in early morning fog,' Tschimpke wrote of the original Somme crossing, 'when, at 4.30 in the morning, the first companies of our rifle regiments rushed across the Somme Bridge in long lines. On the other bank, they immediately develop into a fight. The guns of the German artillery offer their fiery salute to the rising young day. The bank slope rises steeply. To the right and left, on both sides of the village of Flexicourt, the landscape is dotted with green patches of forest. The dirty-grey smoke of exploding grenades billows and hisses from them. Our batteries are taking firing effectively at the innumerable hidden positions of the enemy, which have been reconnoitred by reconnaissance planes. The large calibre projectiles of the French artillery pave the whole wide section. They often struck just before the riflemen of the first German attack wave. Then they lie still for a few seconds, clutching the ground. You listen to the impact and flight direction of the projectiles. Now … continue! They jump into the craters they have just drilled; they climb out. The attack rolls. Now the tanks are continuing it. They eat their way up the slopes in wide waves. They are met with furious artillery fire. Enemy tanks launch a flank attack. The German tanks make a turn, they strike the enemy tanks in the flank.'

A camera pans to where Rommel and staff are sitting on the grass.

Rommel and officers from the 25th Panzer Regiment observe a reconnaissance aircraft passing overhead. Left to right: Major Franz von Lindenau, Oberst Karl Rothenburg, Major Casimir Kentel, possibly Hauptmann Adelbert Schulz, Generalmajor Erwin Rommel, plus Major i.G. Otto Heidkämper.

Rommel monitors the movement in a Sd.Kfz. 251/6 mittlerer Kommandopanzerwagen Ausf A.

Vormarsch! Note the cine camera (far left) beside the 3.7cm Pak; on the right, a Pz.Kpfw. 38(t).

The 6x4 Krupp L2 H 143 (Kfz. 70) Mannschaftstransportwagen (MTW) or troop carrier was produced from 1936 to 1942. Note the low-flying Storch on the left.

A Pz.Kpfw. 38(t) moves through a simulated artillery bombardment towards Hangest. One of the primary functions of the propaganda campaign film was to portray the speed and overwhelming power of the German military. Entertaining the German populace and reinforcing their confidence in Hitler, such films became a psychological weapon against countries who believed they would be attacked next.

German command tanks: Pz.Kpfw. II 'R11' and Panzerbefehlswagen 38(t) 'RO2' with its conspicuous frame antenna. In the original fighting on 5 June, the 7th Panzer Division suffered 68 men killed and 154 wounded.

Hangest-sur-Somme

'Storming the enemy village', the scene of bitter fighting in June 1940. German troops were taught that 'smoke assists the concealment of units. … A deceptive smoke screen can mislead and distract the enemy, attract his fire, and reduce his state of alert. Such a technique only works when the enemy does not recognise it as a deceptive measure.'

During the original battle, Rommel directed a Parzer battalion against the western side of the village to 'shoot up the enemy' without becoming involved in a battle for the village itself.

Shooting the 'fighting' at Hangest-sur-Somme. Against a smoky, atmospheric backdrop, a Pz.Kpfw. I pair advance. (*Personal collection of Barthélémy Vieillot, France – reproduced with kind permission*)

Stills from *Sieg im Westen*. Hangest is 'taken' for the second time.

Another shot in the sequence features a Pz.Kpfw. II Ausf. *B* before the Magasins de l'Economie Menagere building.

Several captured French Tirailleurs and a French second lieutenant were shot after the fighting on 5 June 1940. A French officer later testified: 'The enemy then appears, furious, beside himself, ready to finish us off all together. A German officer intervened to prevent the troops from executing the European officers, but there was no indigenous man alive anymore after a few moments.' Propaganda disseminated by Goebbels at the end of May had already stirred up hatred against France's use of colonial troops, one paper, for example, exclaiming that 'we will no longer tolerate that German soldiers have had their throats cut by coloured soldiers … and that our wounded are murdered in bestial ways. … These murderous beasts will find no pardon.'

Stills from *Sieg im Westen* showing a 15cm sIG 33 auf Pz. I self-propelled gun firing point-blank in Hangest. *Life* magazine (1941) captioned these scenes: 'An assault gun rumbles up to the front line in the French town of Hangest … just south of the river Somme. The house directly ahead is being defended by the French troops. At point-blank range, the assault gun throws a 105mm (4-in) [*sic*] shell at the defended house.' Careful analysis of the film reveals at least three cine cameras positioned in various locations to capture the action.

Storming Château le Quesnoy

Filming the mock attack at Château le Quesnoy, a 35mm cine camera on a tripod capturing the commander's view (see below). Oberst Dr Kurt Hesse, a friend of Rommel's, reassigned Hans Ertl from Propaganda-Kompanie 501 to oversee the re-staged footage. Hesse, an expert on military psychology and psychological warfare, worked tirelessly to form an independent army propaganda branch and was head of Wehrmacht Propaganda Section V – the army's own propaganda organisation, much to the annoyance of Goebbels' Propagandaministerium, which wanted all PK unit footage sent directly to it.

Life (10 March 1941) – 'Germany issues a new thriller entitled *Victory in the West*' – wrote, 'No Hollywood movie was ever more carefully script-written and rehearsed than Germany's conquest of western Europe. What is more astonishing is that the Germans then photographed it almost as if it were just a movie … [it] shows a war brilliantly fought by small combat teams. There is almost no horror, few dead, no agonised wounded.'

This advertisement for *Sieg im Westen* also featured the commander of '321' at Château le Quesnoy.

A Pz.Kpfw. I (minus one machine gun) emerges from a heavily camouflaged position.

A similarly hidden Panzer II Ausf. B (and passenger) also enters the battlefield.

Minus camera crew, Pz.Kpfw. IV '322' moves forward. *Sieg im Westen* depicted the fighting through only a narrow lens of authenticity. Through a clever and skilful combination of editing, narration and music, it distorted reality and gave its audience the illusion of being in the heat of battle as the Wehrmacht crushed all resistance.

Silhouetted, a Pz.Kpfw. II emerges from a watery crossing.

An atmospheric shot of a Pz.Kpfw. 38(t) '212'.

Pz.Kpfw. II and Pz.Kpfw. 38(t).

Rommel's tanks approach the château's masonry wall. Senegalese troops offered significant resistance in the original battle where one battalion had 'installed itself very skilfully' within the walled grounds.

A 15cm sIG 33 auf Pz. I self-propelled gun leads S.Pz.Sp.Wg (Fu) 232 8-Rad and Sd.Kfz. 222 light armoured car.

A Pz.Kpfw. IV fires a 7.5cm Nebelgranate smoke shell. Upon impact, a dense cloud of sulphur trioxide is released, blinding the enemy and aiding the advance. The corrosive nature of the chemical filler necessitated that these rounds were loaded immediately prior to their anticipated use.

Filming progressed smoothly, Ertl recounted, thanks to the 'exemplary organisation' of Rommel, Rothenburg and the 25th Panzer Regiment. After only a few days, 'the most important part of my shooting was in the can'. Later at Abbeville, Rommel winked and (purportedly) remarked to Ertl that 'we may see each other again soon' – a romanticised reference to the forthcoming despatch of an armoured detachment to North Africa.

Pz.Kpfw. 38(t) '121' and '114' roll forward towards Château le Quesnoy.

A Krupp Protze, one of 7,000 built, negotiates the hill towing a 7.5cm leichtes Infanteriegeschütz 18 (7.5cm le IG 18) ('Light Infantry Gun').

The Renault FT (also known as the FT 17) was a light two-man tank developed in 1917. Setting the vehicle alight, an individual disappears to the left.

Propaganda as reality. Another shot from the 1941 book *Entscheidende Stunden – mit der Kamera am Feind* (*Decisive Hours – With the Camera and the Enemy*), showing the armoured attack on the *château* with smoke shells fired for dramatic effect. The masonry wall can be seen in the distance.

Approaching the château's outer masonry wall; Nebelgranate shells explode for the camera.

'Walls are broken.' Filmed from multiple angles, three Pz.Kpfw. IVs burst through the château's masonry wall. Note the censured turret numbers. Rommel recorded that the wall enclosing Château le Quesnoy was defended by a battalion of coloured troops. Stones had been removed to provide loopholes for firing machine and anti-tank guns against the German armour. 'But even here they had no success, for the rapid fire of our tanks, particularly the shells of the Panzer IVs soon smashed the enemy forces.'

With its track repaired, Pz.Kpfw. IV '321' featured prominently in the charge (headlights removed to prevent damage).

321

321

321

321

321

321

Sieg im Westen was completed in mid-January 1941 and shown to Hitler prior to the public premiere on 31 January in Berlin's Ufa-Palast am Zoo. Goebbels commented that it 'has a mass of defects, but the material is so strong that in the end it overwhelms one. The public, mostly officers, was deeply moved.' Reichsmarschall Hermann Göring was dissatisfied with how the Luftwaffe's role was portrayed.

A battalion of French black troops were drafted from POW camps especially for the filming (some 15,000–20,000 were held prisoner at the time). Directions were given to throw away their weapons, raise their arms and yell 'comrade' to the approaching German tanks. However, the 'extras' overacted, screaming in terror. Filming was stopped while Rommel called for a more subdued approach. Several black lives were lost during the re-enactment. Rommel commented on the final day of shooting that 'no expense' had been spared during the filming to portray 'everything was as it really was'.

The turret number of Pz.Kpfw. 38(t) '114' was censored before publication. Imaginatively captioned, the accompanying text states how 'anti-tank projectiles flash by and machine-gun bullets drum against the steel plating but the tanks continue to break through the enemy positions. In panic, the French emerge with raised hands.'

Rommel logged on the final day of shooting how 'there were blacks in it again today. The fellows had a whale of a time and thoroughly enjoyed putting up their hands all over again.' Nevertheless, the scenes featuring the surrender of Senegalese Tirailleurs were cut from the final edit of *Sieg im Westen*. Similarly, there is no reference to the activity in Rommel's *Papers*, which were edited post-war by a respectful Basil Liddell Hart.

Tschimpke's prejudiced account of the original fighting denigrated the defending infantry to 'savage, completely uncivilized primeval forest people with wide tattoo cuts in their raw faces. They fight sneakily, from ever new hidden positions. They would rather be killed than captured. Hand grenades create air. The machine guns are hardly able to be used in the forest. … Many a brave German soldier must give up his life.'

After watching the movie in Libya, Rommel wrote to his wife on 5 March 1941: a 'gala performance of *Sieg im Westen* was given here today. In welcoming the guests – there were a lot – some with wives – I said I hoped the day would come when we'd be showing *Victory in Africa*.' Interestingly, Rommel's adjutant, Hans-Joachim Schräpler, noted the day before how 'a film on the western front and our victory will be shown; the Italian officers and their wives are invited. I know the film. The war is something else, and not as harmless as it is depicted in it.'

Appendix 1

7th Panzer Division Order of Battle, 10 May 1940

Commanding Officer: Generalmajor Erwin Rommel (5 February 1940–14 February 1941)

Ia (Chief Operations Officer): Major i.G. Otto Heidkämper
Ib (Chief Supply Officer): Hauptman i.G. Joachim von Metzsch
Ic (Chief Intelligence Officer): Major i.G Joachim Ziegler
Chief Medical Officer: Dr Wilhelm Baumeister
Chief Orderly: Leutnant der Reserve Karl Hanke

25th Panzer Regiment: Oberst Karl Rothenburg, Panzerregiment 25

I Panzer Battalion: Schmidt/I. Panzerabteilung
II Panzer Battalion: Max Ilgen
III (66th) Panzer Battalion: Major Rudolf Sieckenius

7th Rifle (Schuetzen) Brigade (Oberst Fürst) / 7. Schützenbrigade (Oberst Friedrich Fürst)

6th Rifle Regiment: Oberst Erich von Unger/Schützenregiment 6
I Battalion: Major Paris/I. Abteilung
II Battalion: Oberstleutnant Hans Junck/II. Abteilung
7th Rifle Regiment: Oberst Georg von Bismarck/Schützenregiment 7
I Battalion: Major Hans Cramer
II Battalion: Major Bachmann
705th heavy Infantry Artillery Company/schwere Infanterie-Geschütz-Kompanie (s. Inf GeschKomp 705)

78th Artillery Regiment: 10.5cm (Oberst Gottfried Frölich)/Artillerieregiment 78

I Battalion: Kessler/I. Abteilung
II Battalion: Eduard Crasemann/II. Abteilung
III battalion from 6 June 1940: Hans Joachim von Kronhelm/III. Abteilung

7th Motorcycle Battalion: Major Friedrich-Carl von Steinkeller/Kraftradschützenbataillon 7

37th Armoured Reconnaissance Battalion: Major Günther Erdmann, KIA 28 May 1940 near Capinghem/Panzeraufklärungsabteilung 37, posthumously promoted to Oberstleutnant

42nd Anti-tank Battalion: Oberstleutnant Johann Mickl/Panzerjägerabteilung 42

58th Combat Engineer Battalion, motorised: Major Binkau, KIA 13 May/Pionierbataillon 58
58th Supply Battalion/Nachschubbataillon 58
83rd Communications Battalion: Müller/Nachrichtenabteilung 83
59th light Anti-aircraft Battalion: Major Schrader/Leichte Flakabteilung 59

Appendix 2

1940 Timeline for the 7th Panzer Division in France

10 May	*Fall Gelb* (Case Yellow), the invasion of France, is launched. Rommel crosses the Belgium frontier at Hemmeres, with first enemy contact at Chabrehez.
12 May	The 7th Panzer Division reaches the Meuse River near Dinant and Houx.
13 May	Rommel crosses the Meuse River at two points after heavy fighting.
14 May	The 7th Rifle Regiment captures the village of Onhaye, west of Dinant.
15 May	After reaching Philippeville, Rommel's armour continues west towards Cerfontaine.
16 May	Rommel breaks through the extended Maginot Line.
17 May	The town of Avesnes-sur-Helpe is seized and Rommel's tanks cross the Sambre River into Landrecies.
19 May	Cambrai is occupied.
21 May	The 7th Panzer Division counterattacked by two British armoured regiments at Arras.
28 May	Rommel escapes unscathed from another brush with death in the village of Lomme, west of Lille.
5 June	The 7th Panzer Division crosses the Somme, a battle later recreated for the propaganda film *Sieg im Westen*.
10 June	Rommel arrives at the English Channel at Les Petites-Dalles.
11 June	The 25th Panzer Regiment advances from Veulettes-sur-Mer east towards Saint-Valery-en-Caux.
12 June	The combined French-British force at Saint-Valery-en-Caux surrenders.
15 June	The 7th Panzer Division passes through Le Havre towards Cherbourg.
17 June	The southern outskirts of Cherbourg are reached.
19 June	Cherbourg is declared an open city and surrenders to Rommel.
22 June	A Franco-German armistice is signed. Northern France is to be occupied while the south-east of the country is to remain under the control of Marshal Philippe Petain's government in Vichy.
24 June	The 7th Panzer Division arrives in the port city of Bordeaux on 24 June 1940.

Bibliography

Academic Theses

Moné, T., '15 mai 1940, le mercredi de La Horgne: de la mémoire à l'histoire'. 'La campagne de Mai–Juin 1940 de la 3e Brigade de Spahis', *Histoire* (Université Paris 4 Paris-Sorbonne, 2016).

Foreign Military Studies Office

P-Series, MS # P-040, Mueller-Hillebrand, B. et al., Project #27, The Tank Repair Service in the German Army.

Journal and Magazine Articles

'Germany Issues a New Thriller Entitled *Victory in the West*', *Life* (10 March 1941).

Bernin, M., 'Königstein Prison', *Life* (21 September 1942).

Cooper, G.C., 'Sieg im Westen' [1941]: interservice and bureaucratic propaganda rivalries in Nazi Germany, *Historical Journal of Film, Radio and Television*, Vol. 9, No. 1 (1989).

Kedward, H.R., 'Patriots and Patriotism in Vichy France', *Transactions of the Royal Historical Society*, Vol. 32 (1982), pp. 175–92.

Kirchner, D.P., 'The Early-Modern Seacoast Defenses of Cherbourg', *The Coast Defense Journal*, Vol. 30. Issue 2.

Moné, T., 'Juin 1940 en France: Rommel et la Manipulation de la Mémoire', *La Sabretache* (4 July 2018).

Robinson, J.R., 'The Rommel Myth', *Military Review* LXXVII, No. 5 (September–October 1997).

Sakmyster, T., 'Nazi documentaries of intimidation: "Feldzug in Polen" (1940), "Feuertaufe" (1940) and "Sieg im Westen" (1941)', *Historical Journal of Film, Radio and Television*, Vol. 16, No. 4 (1996), pp. 485–514.

Samuels, M., 'Erwin Rommel and Military Doctrine, 1912–1940', *War in History* 2017, Vol. 24(3), pp. 308–35.

Scheck, R., 'The Killing of Black Soldiers from the French Army by the Wehrmacht in 1940: The Question of Authorization', *German Studies Review*, Vol. 28, No. 3 (October 2005), pp. 595–606.

——, '"They are Just Savages": German Massacres of Black Soldiers from the French Army in 1940', *The Journal of Modern History*, Vol. 77, No. 2 (June 2005), pp. 325–44.

Published Sources

Allcorn, W., *The Maginot Line 1928–45* (Oxford, 2003).
Auphan, P. & Mordal, J., *The French Navy in World War II* (Annapolis, 2016).
Balck, H., *Order in Chaos: The Memoirs of General of Panzer Troops Hermann Balck* (Lexington, 2017).
Bance, A. (Trans.), *Blitzkrieg in their Own Words: First-Hand Accounts from German Soldiers 1939–1940* (London, 2005).
Battistelli, P.P., *Panzer Divisions: The Blitzkrieg Years 1939–40* (Oxford, 2007).
Beckett, I.F.W., *Rommel: A Reappraisal* (Barnsley, 2013).
Beevor, A., *The Second World War* (London, 2013).
Borchert, E., *Entscheidende Stunden – mit der Kamera am Feind* (Berlin, 1941).
Bradford, G., *German Early War Armored Fighting Vehicles* (Mechanicsburg, Pennsylvania, 2006).
Brighton, T., *Masters of Battle: Monty, Patton and Rommel at War* (London, 2008).
Buckton, H., *Retreat: Dunkirk and the Evacuation of Western Europe* (Stroud, Gloucestershire, 2017).
Buffetaut, Y., *Rommel: France 1940* (Bayeux, 1985).
Burdick & Jacobson, *The Halder War Diary 1939–1942* (Novato, California, 1988).
Butler, D.A., *Field Marshal: The Life and Death of Erwin Rommel* (Mechanicsburg, Pennsylvania, 2018).
Caddick-Adams, P., *Monty and Rommel: Parallel Lives* (New York, 2012).
Chant, C., *Artillery* (London, 2005).
Churchill, W., *Their Finest Hour. The Second World War*, Vol. 2 (London, 2005).
Clark, L., *Blitzkrieg: Myth, Reality and Hitler's Lightning War – France, 1940* (London, 2016).
Condell, B. & Zabecki, D.T. (trans & eds), *On the German Art of War: Truppenführung, German Army Manual for Unit Command in World War II* (Mechanicsburg, Pennsylvania, 2009).
Cornwell, P.D., *The Battle of France Then and Now: Six Nations Locked in Aerial Combat September 1939 to June 1940* (Old Harlow, Essex, 2007).
Cras, H., *Les Forces Maritimes du Nord (1939–1940)* (Paris, 1956).
De Gaulle, C., *The Complete War Memoirs of Charles De Gaulle* (New York, 1998).
De Vos, L., *La Belgique et la Seconde Guerre mondiale* (Tielt, Belgium, 2004).
Ditcham, T., *A Home on the Rolling Main: A Naval Memoir 1940–1946* (Barnsley, 2013).
Doughty, R.A., *The Breaking Point: Sedan 1940* (London, 1990).
Eckart, W.U. (ed.), *Man, Medicine, and the State: The Human Body as an Object of Government-Sponsored Medical Research in the 20th Century* (Stuttgart, 2006).
Evans, M.M., *The Fall of France: Act with Daring* (Oxford, 2000).
Fletcher, D., *Universal Carrier 1936–48: The 'Bren Gun Carrier' Story* (Oxford, 2005).
Forczyk, R. *Case Red: The Collapse of France* (Oxford, 2017).
Frieser, K-H., *The Blitzkrieg Legend: The 1940 Campaign in the West* (Annapolis, 2005).
Giesen, R., *Nazi Propaganda Films: A History and Filmography* (Jefferson, North Carolina, 2003).

Grehan, J. & Mace., M., *The BEF in France 1939–1940: Manning the Front Through to the Dunkirk Evacuation* (Barnsley, 2014).
Guest, P., *Wilfred Owen: On the Trail of the Poets of the Great War* (Barnsley, 2001).
Hart, C. et al., *World War II & the Media. A Collection of Essays* (Chester, 2014).
Higgins, D.R., *Panzer II vs 7TP: Poland 1939* (Oxford, 2015).
Hoffman, H., *The Triumph of Propaganda: Film and National Socialism, 1933–1945* (New York, 1997).
Hogg, I.V., *German Artillery of World War Two* (Mechanicsburg, Pennsylvania, 1997).
Home, A., *To Lose a Battle: France 1940* (London, 2007).
Horne, J.N. & Kramer, A., *German Atrocities, 1914: A History of Denial* (New Haven, 2001).
Innes, B. (ed.), *St Valery: The Impossible Odds* (Edinburgh, 2004).
Irving, D., *The Trail of the Fox: The Life of Field-Marshal Erwin Rommel* (Hertfordshire, 1977).
Jackson, J., *The Fall of France: The Nazi Invasion of 1940* (Oxford, 2003).
Jentz, T.L., *Panzertruppen: The Complete Guide to the Creation & Combat Employment of Germany's Tank Force 1933–1942* (Atglen, Pennsylvania, 1996).
Kallis, A., *Nazi Propaganda and the Second World War* (Basingstoke, 2005).
Kamienski L., *Shooting Up: A History of Drugs in Warfare* (London, 2017).
Kaufmann, J.E. et al., *The Maginot Line: History and Guide* (Barnsley, 2011).
Kaufmann, J.E. & Kaufmann, H.W., *Fortress France: The Maginot Line and French Defenses in World War II* (Mechanicsburg, Pennsylvania, 2007).
Kemp, A., *The Maginot Line: Myth and Reality* (London, 1981).
Kershaw, R., *Tank Men: The Human Side of Tanks at War* (London, 2008).
Kistler, J., *Animals in the Military: From Hannibal's Elephants to the Dolphins of the US Navy* (Santa Barbara, 2011).
Lemay, B., *Erwin Rommel* (Paris, 2009).
Lewin, R., *Rommel as Military Commander* (New York, 1968).
Liddell Hart, B.H. (ed.), *The Rommel Papers* (London, 1953).
Lipkes, J., *Rehearsals: The German Army in Belgium, August 1914* (Florida, 2014).
Longden, S., *Dunkirk: The Men They Left Behind* (London, 2009).
Lorimer, D., *Bordeaux brûle-t-il?, ou, La libération de la Gironde: 1940–1945* (Bordeaux, 1998).
Maier, K.A. et al., *Germany and the Second World War*, Volume II, *Germany's Initial Conquests in Europe* (Oxford, 1991).
Mary, J-Y., *Mémorial de la Bataille de France*: Volume 4, *Du 17 au 25 Juin 1940* (Bayeux, 2018).
Mitcham, S.W., *Rommel's Lieutenants: The Men Who Served the Desert Fox, France, 1940* (Santa Barbara, 2006).
——, *Hitler's Legions: The German Army Order of Battle, World War II* (New York, 1985).
Mitchelhill-Green, D., *Tobruk 1942* (Stroud, Gloucestershire, 2016).
Nijboer, D., *Flak in World War II* (Mechanicsburg, Pennsylvania, 2018).
Nobécourt, R.G., *Les soldats de 40 dans la première bataille de Normandie, de la Bresle au Cotentin 5–19 Juin 1940* (Luneray, 1986).
Ohler, N., *Blitzed: Drugs in Nazi Germany* (London, 2017).
Pallud, J.P., *Blitzkrieg in the West: Then and Now* (London, 1991).
Perrett, B., *Iron Fist: Classic Armoured Warfare* (London, 2012).
Romanych, M. & Rupp, M., *Maginot Line 1940: Battles on the French Frontier* (Oxford, 2010).

Reuth, R.G., *Rommel:The End of the Legend* (London, 2004).
Scheck, R., *Hitler's African Victims: The German Army Massacres of Black French Soldiers in 1940* (Cambridge, 2008).
——, *French Colonial Soldiers in German Captivity during World War II* (Cambridge, 2018).
Schraepler, H.A. (ed.), *At Rommel's Side:The Lost Letters of Han Joachim Schraepler* (London, 2009).
Sebag-Montefiore, H., *Dunkirk: Fight to the Last Man* (London, 2007).
Shennan, A.W.H., *The Fall of France, 1940* (Abingdon, 2017).
Smithers, A.J., *Cambrai:The First Great Tank Battle* (London, 1992).
Stahlberg, A., *Bounden Duty:The Memoirs of a German Officer 1932–45* (London, 1990).
Stolfi, R.H.S., *The 7th Panzer Division in France and Russia: Rommel's Ghost Division* (Barnsley, 2014).
Thomas, M. (ed.), *The French Colonial Mind,* Vol. 2: *Violence, Military Encounters and Colonialism* (Lincoln, Nebraska, 2012).
Thomas, N., *The German Army 1939–45 (1): Blitzkrieg* (Oxford, 1997).
Trevor-Roper, H.R. (ed.), *Hitler's War Directives 1939–1945* (London, 1964).
Tschimpke, A., *Die Gespenster-Division. Mit der Panzerwaffe durch Belgien und Frankreich* (Munich, 1940).
Uziel, D., *The Propaganda Warriors:The Wehrmacht and the Consolidation of the German Home Front* (Bern, 2008).
Vanderveen, B., *Historic Military Vehicles Directory* (London, 1989).
Von Luck, H., *Panzer Commander* (New York, 1989).
Von Mellenthin, F.W., *Panzer Battles* (New York, 1956).
Von Moltke, J., *The Curious Humanist: Siegfried Kracauer in America* (Berkeley, California, 2016).
Welch, D., *Propaganda and the German Cinema, 1933–1945* (Oxford, 1983).
Wernick, R., *Blitzkrieg* (Alexandria, Virginia, 1977).
Westphal, S., *The German Army in the West* (London, 1951).
Zaloga, S.J., *Panzer 38(t)* (Oxford, 2014).
——, *Cherbourg 1944:The first Allied victory in Normandy* (Oxford, 2015).
——, *Panzer IV vs Char B1 bis: France 1940* (Oxford, 2011).

Websites

http://51hd.co.uk
http://www.chars-francais.net

Film and Television

Svend Noldan et al. (dir.), *Sieg im Westen (Victory in the West)*, Berlin, 1941.
The Other Side of Dunkirk, BBC, 2004.

Further Titles by the Same Author:

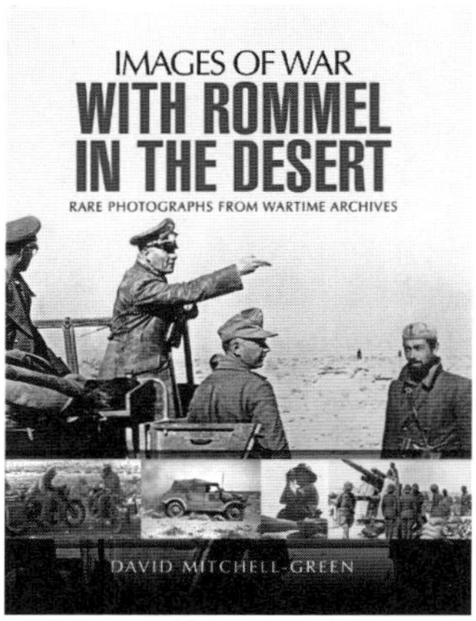

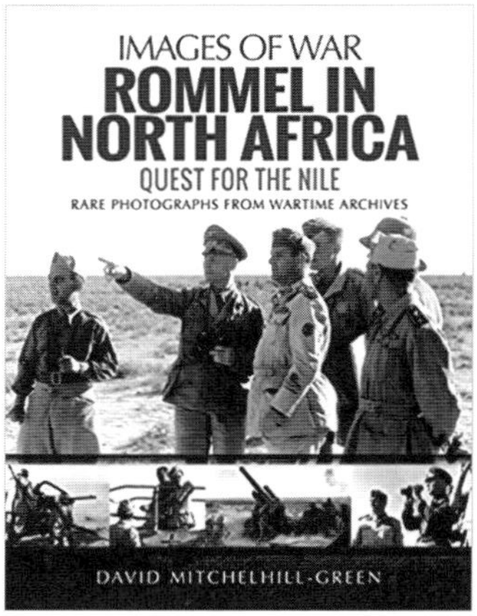

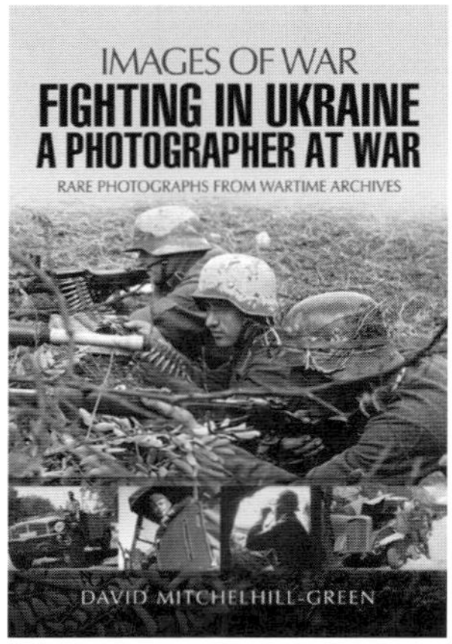

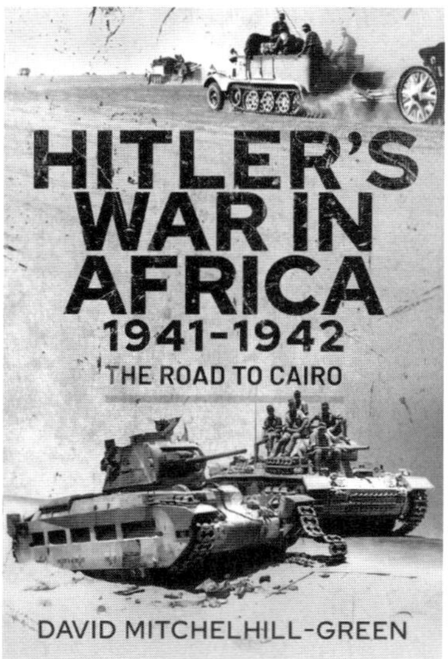

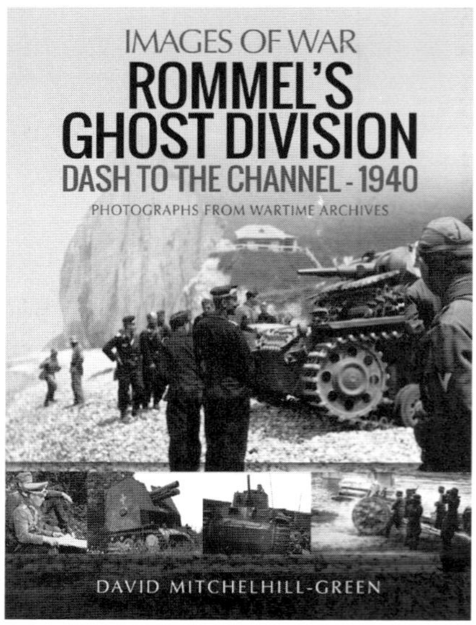